This revision and classroom companion is matched to the new **OCR GCSE Biology Specification** (**J633**), from the Twenty First Century Science Suite.*

As a revision guide, this book focuses on the skills and material on which you will be examined. It does not cover the practical data analysis and case study (Unit 4) or the practical investigation (Unit 5), which will be internally assessed by your science teacher and count for 33.3% of your total mark.

All seven modules from the specification are covered in this guide. You will need to study, and sit exams for, **all** of these modules.

An overview of the exams for OCR GCSE Biology A is provided below, with details of where the relevant material can be found in this guide.

The Ideas in Context exam paper will focus on the ideas covered in all of the modules you have studied. It will test your knowledge of the content and your ability to apply that knowledge, for example, to evaluate information about a current social–science issue effectively. This paper is looked at in more detail on pages 85–90 of this revision guide.

The **contents list and page headers** in this revision guide clearly identify the separate modules, to help you to revise for the different exam papers.

This guide can be used to revise for both the Foundation and Higher Tier exam papers.

> **HT** Content that will only be tested on the Higher Tier papers appears in a coloured box, and can easily be identified by the Higher Tier symbol **HT**.

- You will find a **glossary** at the end of the book providing clear definitions of essential words and phrases.

- Don't just read the information in this guide – **learn actively**! Jot down anything you think will help you to remember, no matter how trivial it may seem, and constantly test yourself without looking at the text.

Good luck in your exams!

*All material correct at time of going to print.

Title	What is Being Assessed?	How it is Assessed	Weighting	Total Mark	Page No.
Unit 1	B1, B2, B3	40 minutes written paper	16.7%	42	4–33
Unit 2	B4, B5, B6	40 minutes written paper	16.7%	42	34–59
Unit 3	B7 and Ideas in Context	60 minutes written paper	33.3%	55	60–90
Unit 4 **OR**	Practical Data Analysis and Case Study	Assessed internally	33.3%	40	——
Unit 5	Practical Investigation	Assessed internally	33.3%	40	——

Unit 1

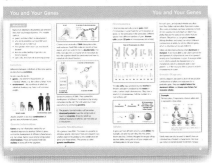

Unit 2

Unit 3

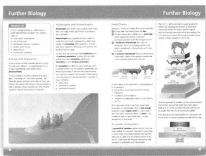

Contents

Contents

You and Your Genes

Many of an individual's characteristics are inherited from their two biological parents. This module looks at…

- genes, and their effect on development
- why family members can resemble each other but are not identical
- how genetic information can, and should, be used
- how an understanding of genetics can prevent disease
- stem cells, and their role in treating disease.

Variation

Differences between individuals of the same species are described as **variations**.

Variation may be due to…
- **genes** – the different characteristics an individual inherits, e.g. the colour of dogs' coats
- **environment** – the conditions in which an individual develops, e.g. how much someone weighs.

Genetic causes   **Environmental causes**

Usually variation is due to a **combination** of genetic and environmental causes.

Genetic Information

Genes carry the information needed for an individual organism to develop. Different genes control the development of different characteristics, e.g. eye colour. Genes occur in long strings called **chromosomes**. These are located inside the **nucleus** of every cell in the organism.

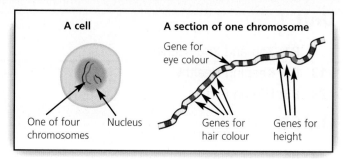

A cell	A section of one chromosome

Gene for eye colour

One of four chromosomes   Nucleus   Genes for hair colour   Genes for height

Chromosomes are made of **DNA** (deoxyribonucleic acid) molecules. Each DNA molecule consists of two strands, which are coiled to form a **double helix**. The DNA molecules form a complete set of instructions for how the organism should be constructed and how its individual cells should function.

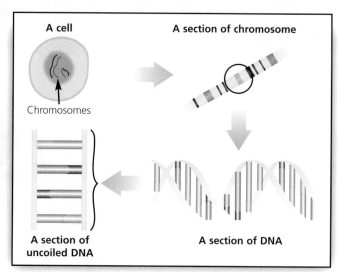

A cell   A section of chromosome

Chromosomes

A section of uncoiled DNA   A section of DNA

Genes are sections of DNA. They control the development of different characteristics by issuing instructions to the cell. The cell carries out these instructions by producing **proteins**.

(HT) The proteins formed inside a cell are either **structural proteins** (used for cell growth or repair) or **enzymes**. Enzymes speed up chemical reactions in cells but are not used up in the process.

Genetic Modification

All organisms have DNA. This means it is possible to introduce genetic information from one organism into another organism to produce a new combination of genes and characteristics. This process is called **genetic modification**.

Chromosomes

Chromosomes normally come in **pairs**. Both chromosomes in a pair have the same sequence of genes, i.e. the same genes in the same place. Different species have different numbers of pairs. **Human cells** contain **23 pairs** of chromosomes (46 in total).

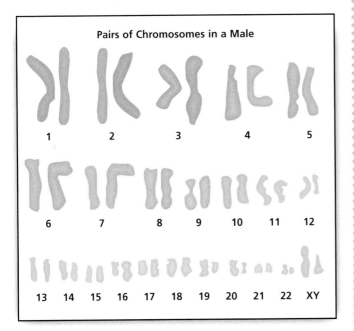

The **sex cells,** eggs produced by the **ovaries** in females and sperm produced by the **testes** in males, contain single chromosomes. They have a total of 23 chromosomes; half the number of a normal body cell.

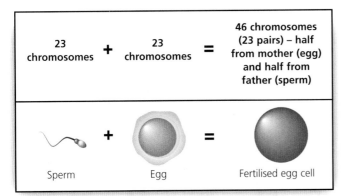

Alleles

A gene can have different versions, called **alleles**. For example, the gene for eye colour has two alleles: brown and blue. Similarly, the gene for tongue rolling has two alleles: being able to roll your tongue and not being able to roll your tongue.

For each gene, an individual inherits one allele from their father and one allele from their mother. (This is why individuals can have similarities to both of their parents.) An individual can inherit two alleles that are the same or two alleles that are different. The process is completely **random**. Siblings (brothers and sisters) can inherit different combinations of alleles for all the different genes, which is why they can be very different.

Alleles are described as being either **dominant** or **recessive**. A dominant allele is one which controls the development of a characteristic even if it is present on only one chromosome in a pair. A recessive allele is one which controls the development of a characteristic only if a dominant allele is not present, i.e. if the recessive allele is present on both chromosomes in a pair.

Genetic Diagrams

Genetic diagrams are used to show all the possible combinations of alleles and outcomes for a particular gene. They use **capital letters for dominant alleles** and **lower case letters for recessive alleles**.

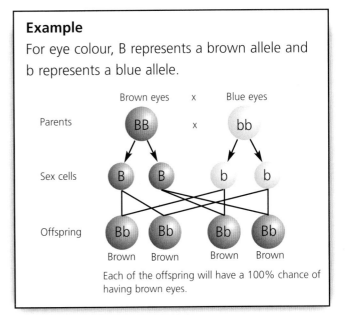

Family trees can also be used to identify how an individual has inherited a characteristic, like blue eye colour or not being able to roll their tongue.

You and Your Genes

Genetics and Lifestyle

Most characteristics are determined by several genes working together, however, they can also be influenced by environmental factors.

For example, height is determined by a variety of genes, but factors like diet can also affect how tall an individual grows.

Factors like poor diet can also lead to disease, e.g. a fatty diet can increase the risk of heart disease.

So, it is possible to limit the chances of getting certain diseases and disorders by making lifestyle changes.

Sex Chromosomes

One of the 23 pairs of chromosomes in a human cell is the sex chromosomes. In females the **sex chromosomes** are identical; they are both **X chromosomes**. In males they are different; there is an **X** and a **Y chromosome**. The Y chromosome is much shorter than the X chromosome.

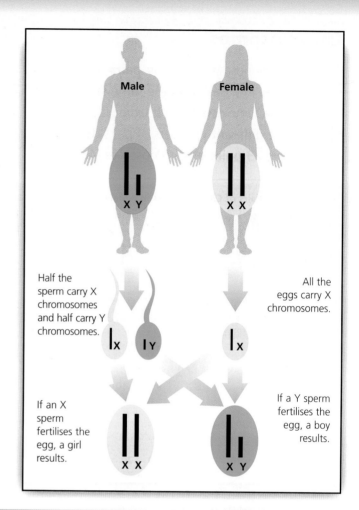

Half the sperm carry X chromosomes and half carry Y chromosomes.

All the eggs carry X chromosomes.

If an X sperm fertilises the egg, a girl results.

If a Y sperm fertilises the egg, a boy results.

Sex Determination

The sex of an individual is determined by a gene on the Y chromosome called the SRY (sex-determining region Y) gene.

If the gene is not present, i.e. if there are two X chromosomes present, the embryo will develop into a female. If the gene is present, i.e. if there are an X and a Y chromosome, testes begin to develop.

After six weeks the testes start producing a hormone called **androgen**. Specialised receptors in the developing embryo detect the androgen and male reproductive organs begin to grow.

Sometimes the Y chromosome is present but androgen is *not* detected. When this happens, the embryo develops all the female sex organs except the uterus. The baby is born with a female body but is infertile.

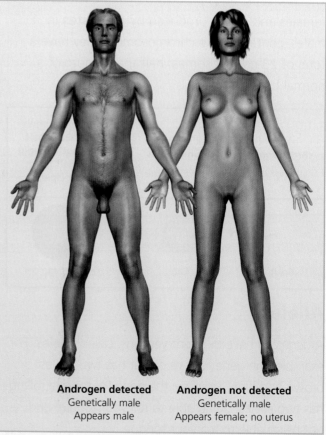

Androgen detected
Genetically male
Appears male

Androgen not detected
Genetically male
Appears female; no uterus

Rare Disorders

Most characteristics are governed by a range of genes, so the presence of one 'faulty' allele may not affect the overall outcome.

However, although rare, there are some disorders which are caused by a single allele, e.g. **Huntington's disorder**.

Huntington's Disorder

Huntington's disorder (HD), is a genetic disorder that affects the **central nervous system**. It is caused by a 'faulty' gene on the fourth pair of chromosomes.

The HD gene results in damage to the nerve cells in certain areas of the brain. This causes gradual physical, mental and emotional changes, which develop into continuous, involuntary movement and dementia. The **symptoms** can differ from person to person, even within the same family.

The initial symptoms of HD normally develop in adulthood, which means sufferers may already have had children and passed on the gene. There is no cure, so the disorder will eventually lead to premature death.

Everyone who inherits the HD gene will, at some stage, develop the disorder. This is because the allele that causes HD is **dominant**. Therefore, only *one* parent needs to pass on the faulty gene for a child to inherit the disorder.

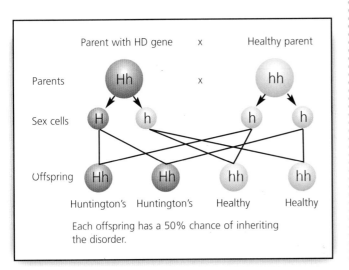

Each offspring has a 50% chance of inheriting the disorder.

Cystic Fibrosis

Cystic fibrosis is the UK's most common life-threatening **genetic disorder**. It affects the cell membranes, causing a **thick**, **sticky** mucus, especially in the **lungs**, **gut** and **pancreas**.

Symptoms of cystic fibrosis can include weight loss, troublesome coughs, repeated chest infections, salty sweat and abnormal faeces.

Although there is no cure at present, scientists have identified the allele that causes it and are looking for ways to repair or replace it.

Unlike Huntington's disorder, the cystic fibrosis allele is **recessive**. Therefore, if an individual has *one* recessive allele, they *will not* have the characteristics associated with the disorder. However, they are called **carriers** because they can pass the allele on to their children.

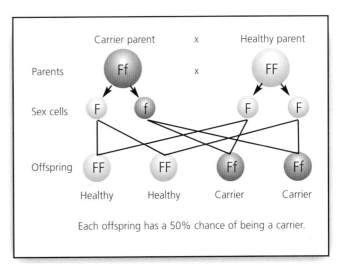

Each offspring has a 50% chance of being a carrier.

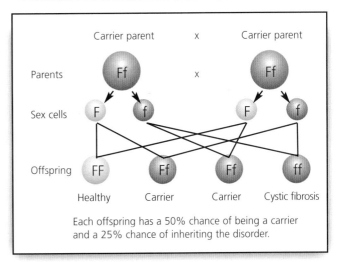

Each offspring has a 50% chance of being a carrier and a 25% chance of inheriting the disorder.

You and Your Genes

Genetic Testing

It is now possible to test individuals for a 'faulty' allele if there is a family history of a genetic disorder. If the tests turn out to be positive, the individual will have to decide whether or not to have children and risk passing on the disorder. Possible alternatives include adoption or embryo selection (see p.9).

Fetuses can also be tested. However, if a developing baby is found to have the faulty allele, the parents then have to decide whether or not to terminate the pregnancy (have an abortion). These decisions can be very difficult and traumatic.

Testing the Fetus

There are two types of genetic test that can be carried out on a fetus.

1 Amniocentesis Testing

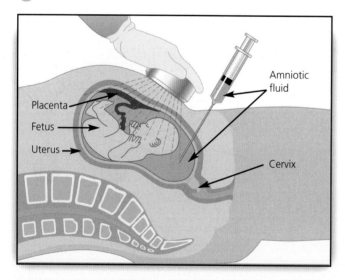

This test can be carried out at 14–16 weeks of pregnancy. A needle is inserted into the uterus, taking care to avoid the fetus and a small sample of amniotic fluid, which carries cells from the fetus, is extracted.

Results take up to two weeks to return. If the test is positive for a given disorder the pregnancy (now at 16–18 weeks) could be terminated. There is a 0.5% chance of the test causing a miscarriage, i.e. 1 in every 200 tests. There is also a very small chance of infection.

2 Chorionic Villus Testing

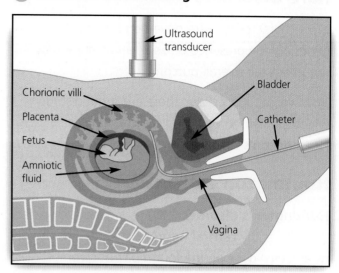

This test is carried out earlier, at 8–10 weeks of pregnancy. A special catheter is inserted through the vagina and cervix until it reaches the placenta. Part of the placenta has chorionic villi (finger-like protrusions), which are made from fetal cells. Samples are removed for testing.

Results take up to two weeks to return. If the test is positive for a given disorder the pregnancy can be terminated much earlier (10–12 weeks) than with amniocentesis testing. However, the chance of a miscarriage is much higher at 2%, i.e. 1 in every 50 tests. There is virtually no risk of infection.

Reliability

Because no test is 100% reliable, genetic testing on a fetus can have a number of possible outcomes:

Outcome	Test result	Reality
True Positive	Fetus has the disorder	Fetus has the disorder
True Negative	Fetus does not have the disorder	Fetus does not have the disorder
False Positive	Fetus has the disorder	Fetus **does not** have the disorder
False Negative	Fetus does not have the disorder	Fetus **has** the disorder

False negatives are rare and false positives are even rarer. However, the consequence of a false positive is that the parents may choose to terminate the pregnancy when the fetus is in fact healthy.

The Implications of Genetic Testing

There are lots of questions that need to be addressed before genetic testing can become common practice. For example:

- How can we prevent mistakes from being made?
- Is it right to interfere with nature in this way?
- How can we decide, and who has the right to decide, if a genetic disorder is worth living with?

There is always a difference between what **can** be done (i.e. what is technically possible) and what **should** be done (i.e. what is morally acceptable). For example, governments may have the ability to genetically test individuals, but should they be allowed to do so?

Potentially, genetic testing could be used to produce detailed genetic profiles. These could contain information on everything from an individual's ethnicity to whether they are susceptible to certain conditions (e.g. obesity) or diseases (e.g. cancer).

It has been suggested that all babies could be screened at birth, allowing doctors to tailor healthcare for the individual and take action to prevent problems before they occur. The information could also help to stop genetic disorders from being passed on, eventually eliminating them from the population completely.

One view is that this would be a good thing; there would be less suffering and money currently spent on treating the disorders could be used elsewhere. Another view is that these disorders are natural and that it would be wrong to eliminate them.

The storage of genetic information also raises questions about confidentiality. There are concerns that without tight laws and regulations in place, companies could use the information to discriminate against individuals,

e.g. an individual might be turned down for a job or refused insurance because they have a high risk of getting cancer or heart disease.

Different cultures and societies will have different needs and views on the subject. Because the availability of resources (e.g. money and trained personnel) affects what can be done, different countries also need to develop different policies towards genetic testing depending on their economy.

Embryo Selection

Embryo selection is another way of preventing babies from being born with genetic disorders.

Embryos can be produced by *in vitro* **fertilisation** (IVF). This is when ova (egg cells) are **harvested** from the mother, and fertilised in a laboratory using the father's sperm. The embryos are tested to see if they have a 'faulty' allele. Only the healthy ones are implanted into the mother's uterus, and the pregnancy then proceeds as normal.

The procedure for embryo selection is called **Pre-implantation Genetic Diagnosis (PGD)**.

After fertilisation, the embryos are allowed to divide into 8 cells before a single cell is removed from each one for another testing. The cells are tested to see if they carry the alleles for a specific genetic disorder, i.e. the disorder that one of the parents carries or has.

Embryo selection is controversial. Some people disagree with it because they believe it is unnatural. There are also concerns that people could start using this method to select the characteristics (such as eye colour, sex and IQ) of their baby in advance.

If this is allowed to happen it could reduce variation in humans. For example, if most people selected blue eyes, the brown eye allele could eventually disappear from the population.

You and Your Genes

Gene Therapy

Gene therapy is a potential new treatment for certain genetic disorders. It involves inserting 'healthy' genes into an individual's cells to treat a disease.

The most common method uses genes from healthy individuals. They are inserted into a modified virus, which infects the patient. The genes become incorporated into the patient's cells, correcting the faulty allele.

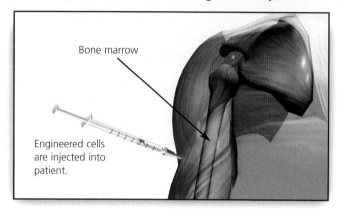

Bone marrow

Engineered cells are injected into patient.

New scientific procedures, like gene therapy, always raise lots of questions:

- Does it work and is it safe?
- What are the potential risks and side effects?
- How do you target the cells that need gene therapy?
- Can gene therapy cause cancer?

These questions can be answered by conducting further scientific research, however, there are some questions that cannot be answered by science:

- Is it right to manipulate genes in this way?
- Where do we draw the line between repairing damage and making improvements?
- Do we have the right to decide for future generations?

These examples are all asking the same basic question: **is gene therapy acceptable**? This is an **ethical** question. To answer it we need to make a value judgement, i.e. decide what is right and wrong.

Society is underpinned by a common belief system. For this reason, there are certain actions that can never be justified. For example, most people agree that theft and murder is wrong.

However, science can be a grey area. Individuals are influenced by different beliefs and experiences, so there are always lots of different views about what is acceptable, and what should be done.

An important question that is in dispute and needs to be settled is called an **issue**. There are lots of different views on most issues. Here are just a few for **gene therapy**:

For

- It is an acceptable medical procedure, comparable to giving a vaccination, and is less invasive than surgery.
- People with genetic conditions often require a lifetime of care and treatment. Gene therapy will improve their lives and will free up resources so they can be used elsewhere.
- Some genetic conditions reduce life expectancy. Gene therapy will allow sufferers to enjoy a full and normal life.

Against

- It is unnatural, and therefore morally wrong, to change people's genes and DNA.
- It is an experimental treatment and we do not know what the long-term effects might be.
- It will need to be tested on humans, which is not safe because we do not know what the side effects are.

An individual cannot decide whether gene therapy is right or wrong by simply counting up the arguments for and against. Each argument will have a different weighting depending on how important it is to them. For example, they might believe that it is far more important to save lives than to worry about the procedure being unnatural.

Because of all the different views, any decisions made by authorities (e.g. governments) over ethical issues are normally based on what will benefit the majority of people involved. Of course, this means there will always be some people who object.

Asexual Reproduction

Bacteria and other single-cell organisms can reproduce by dividing to form two 'new' individuals. The new individuals are **clones** (they are genetically **identical** to the parent).

This method of reproduction is called **asexual reproduction**. Most plants and some animals can also reproduce in this way.

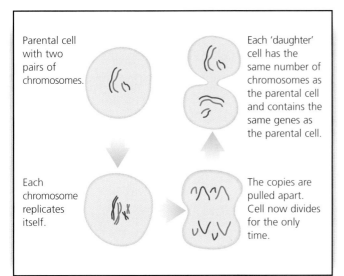

Parental cell with two pairs of chromosomes.

Each 'daughter' cell has the same number of chromosomes as the parental cell and contains the same genes as the parental cell.

Each chromosome replicates itself.

The copies are pulled apart. Cell now divides for the only time.

Variation in organisms that reproduce asexually is normally caused by **environmental factors**.

Clones

Clones of animals and humans can occur **naturally**. The cells of an embryo sometimes separate and the two new embryos develop into **identical twins**.

> **HT** Animal clones can also be produced **artificially**. The nucleus from an adult body cell is transferred into an empty (nucleus removed) unfertilised egg cell. The new individual will therefore have exactly the same genetic information as the donor.

Stem Cells

Most organisms are made up of lots of different **specialised** cells, which have different structures to help them perform their particular jobs.

In the initial stages of development, the cells in an embryo are not yet specialised; they are all the same. These are called **stem cells** and they have the potential to develop into virtually any type of body cell.

Stem cells can potentially be used to replace tissues that are damaged, e.g. they can be inserted into the brain of a patient with Parkinson's disease to replace the cells affected by the disease and alleviate the symptoms.

To produce the large number of stem cells needed for such treatments, it is necessary to clone embryos. The stem cells are collected when the embryo is five days old and made up of approximately 150 cells. The rest of the embryo is destroyed. At the moment, unused embryos from IVF treatments are used for stem cell research.

The Ethical Issue

There is an **issue** as to whether it is right to clone embryos and extract stem cells in this way. The debate revolves around whether or not these embryos should be treated as people. If they should, then using embryos in this way is obviously wrong. If they should not, then the procedure is acceptable.

One view is that if an embryo is produced for IVF treatment but is not used for implantation, it no longer has a future. Therefore, it is acceptable to use it for stem cell research as long as the mother and father have given consent.

However, if these embryos were not available, it has been suggested that embryos could be cloned from the patient's own cells. This is the first stage in **reproductive cloning** (the production of a new individual who is genetically identical to the donor), which is currently illegal in the UK.

The Government makes laws on issues like this with the guidance of special advisory committees, who are responsible for exploring the ethics of such procedures.

You and Your Genes – Summary

Science Explanations

Cells

- Most organisms are made up of specialised cells, which have different structures to help them perform a specific function.

Gene Theory

- Most animals and plants reproduce by sexual reproduction.
- During sexual reproduction a male sex cell joins with a female sex cell to form a fertilised egg.
- Variation (differences) between individuals in a species is caused by genes and the environment.
- The instructions for how an organism will develop are provided by genes.
- Each gene affects a specific characteristic.
- Genes are found in the nuclei of an organism's cells.
- Genes are sections of DNA molecules, which make up chromosomes.
- Chromosomes occur in pairs, except in the sex cells.
- One chromosome in a pair comes from the father and the other from the mother.
- Both chromosomes in a pair carry the same genes in the same place.
- A particular gene can occur in slightly different forms, called alleles.
- A pair of chromosomes can have the same or different alleles for a particular gene.
- If a dominant allele is present it will control the characteristic.
- A recessive allele will control the characteristic only if it is present on both chromosomes.
- The offspring of the same parents can be very different because they inherit different combinations of alleles.
- Cells make proteins by following the instructions provided by genes.
- All organisms use the same genetic code.
- Genetic modification involves the genes from one organism being artificially introduced into another.

- Bacteria and some plants and animals can reproduce asexually.
- Asexual reproduction involves the division of cells to produce new cells.
- Cells produced through asexual reproduction contain exactly the same genetic information.
- New individuals produced asexually are genetically identical to the parent. They are called clones.
- Any differences between these individuals and the parent are due only to the environment.
- The cells of multicellular organisms become specialised in the early stages of development.

Ideas about Science

Making Decisions

- Some questions cannot be answered by science.
- Ethical issues are concerned with what is morally right and wrong.
- Because people have different beliefs and experiences, there are often lots of different views on ethical issues.
- A common argument is that the 'right' decision is the one that leads to the best outcome for the majority of people involved.
- People may disagree with scientific procedures because they feel that they are unnatural or wrong.
- Some people think it is unfair that an individual can benefit from something which was only made possible because others took a risk, when they would not be prepared to take the same risk themselves.

> **HT**
> - There is often a significant difference between what *can* be done and what *should* be done.
> - Different decisions on the same issue may be made in different social and economic contexts.

Keeping Healthy

Module B2

To stay healthy it is important to maintain a healthy lifestyle, practise good hygiene, and use medication when appropriate, e.g. to help prevent or treat illness. This module looks at...

- how our bodies resist infection
- what vaccines are and how they work
- what antibiotics are and why they can become less effective
- how new drugs are developed and tested
- what factors increase the risk of heart disease.

Infection

Infections are caused by harmful **microorganisms**. These microorganisms are divided into **three** groups:

Bacteria
e.g. bubonic plague, tuberculosis (TB), cystitis. Treated by antibiotics.

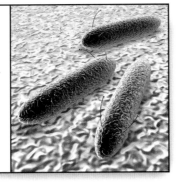

Fungi
e.g. athlete's foot, thrush, ringworm. Treated by anti-fungal medicine and antibiotics.

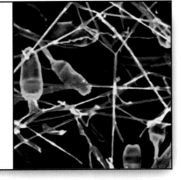

Viruses
e.g. H5N1 (Asian bird flu), common cold, HIV (Human Immunodeficiency Virus), measles, smallpox. Very difficult to treat.

The Body's Defence System

A huge number of microorganisms can be found on any surface and in the air that we breathe. However, the human body has a **defence system,** made up of **physical** and **chemical** barriers, which stops us getting ill all the time:

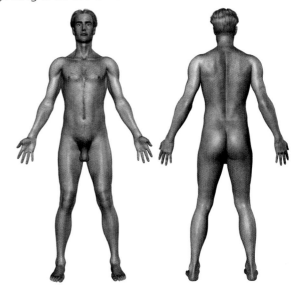

- The skin forms a physical barrier against invasion.
- Chemicals in sweat stop microorganisms from growing on the skin.
- Tears contain chemicals which kill microorganisms to stop them entering through the eye.
- The stomach produces hydrochloric acid which kills microorganisms that get into the food we eat.

The body provides the ideal conditions for microorganisms to thrive; it is warm with plenty of nutrients and moisture. Therefore, if harmful microorganisms do manage to get into the body they reproduce very rapidly – doubling in number every 20 minutes.

When the microorganisms first enter the body there are no symptoms of illness. Only when there is a significant amount of infection do the symptoms (e.g. nausea, pain or a rash) start to show.

These symptoms are caused by the microorganisms in one of two ways:
- by damaging infected cells in some way, e.g. bursting
- by producing harmful poisons (toxins).

Keeping Healthy

The Immune Response

If microorganisms do manage to break through the body's external defences, the **immune system** (the body's internal defence system) is activated to fight the invasion.

White blood cells play a major role in this response:

1 One type of white blood cell moves around the body in the bloodstream looking for microorganisms. When it finds some, it **engulfs** (flows around) them. It then **digests** the microorganism so that it is completely destroyed.

This type of defence occurs when we get a cut and pus develops. The yellow liquid is mainly white blood cells which are full of digested microorganisms.

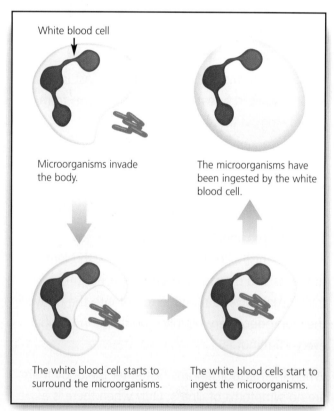

White blood cell

Microorganisms invade the body.

The microorganisms have been ingested by the white blood cell.

The white blood cell starts to surround the microorganisms.

The white blood cells start to ingest the microorganisms.

2 A different type of white blood cell makes special substances called **antibodies** to combat infection. It takes time for white blood cells in the body to produce antibodies. This delay means that microorganisms continue to grow and cause illness (and sometimes death) before they are destroyed.

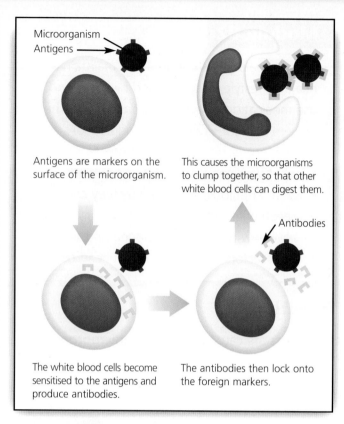

Microorganism
Antigens

Antigens are markers on the surface of the microorganism.

This causes the microorganisms to clump together, so that other white blood cells can digest them.

Antibodies

The white blood cells become sensitised to the antigens and produce antibodies.

The antibodies then lock onto the foreign markers.

Specialisation of Antibodies

Different diseases are caused by different microorganisms. Each microorganism has its own unique markers, called antigens, on its surface.

White blood cells produce antibodies specific to the type of marker they need to attack. This means, for example, that antibodies produced to fight tetanus will have no effect on TB or cholera because they have different markers.

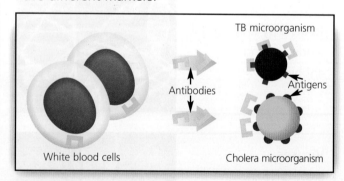

TB microorganism

Antibodies

Antigens

White blood cells

Cholera microorganism

When a person has had an infectious disease, the white blood cells 'remember' the antigens on the surface of the microorganism. As a result, they can produce antibodies quicker if they encounter the same microorganism again. This helps to protect the person against that particular disease and is called **natural immunity**.

Vaccination

Vaccination helps the body to develop long-term immunity against a disease, i.e. produce specific antibodies. So, if the microorganism that causes the disease enters the body, it will be destroyed before any damage is done:

1 Injection of vaccine

A weakened or dead strain of the disease-causing microorganism, which is incapable of multiplying, is injected.

2 Immune response triggered

Although the microorganism is modified, the antigens on its surface still cause the white blood cells to produce specific antibodies.

3 White blood cells remain in bloodstream

Long after the microorganism has been destroyed, white blood cells capable of attacking it remain in the bloodstream. If they come across the same antigen again, they can produce the right antibody much faster than they would if they had not encountered the microorganism before.

Side Effects

Vaccinations are never completely safe. They can produce **side effects** in some individuals. Most side effects are **minor**, e.g. a mild fever or rash, compared to the disease the vaccination is designed to prevent. However, some individuals are affected more than others.

More **extreme** side effects, e.g. encephalitis (inflammation of the brain) or convulsions, are **rare**.

With the controversial MMR (Measles, Mumps and Rubella) vaccination, the chances of getting encephalitis as a side effect are 1 in 1 000 000.

The risk of getting it from measles itself is between 1 in 200 and 1 in 5000 – much higher!

Mutating Viruses

Some vaccines are only effective for a limited period of time because viruses (e.g. influenza) can **mutate** (change) to produce a new **strain** (variety). As a result, new vaccines have to be developed regularly.

For example, flu vaccinations need to be renewed annually because every year a new strain of the virus will be around.

HT **HIV** (**Human Immunodeficiency Virus**), is a virus that attacks the immune system and which can lead to **AIDS** (**Acquired Immune Deficiency Syndrome**). Infected people often die from illnesses that a healthy person can fight off easily, e.g. the common cold.

HIV can be carried for many years without the infected person realising, because they have no symptoms. However, during this period the disease can accidentally be passed on to others.

It is extremely difficult to make an effective vaccine for HIV because…

- **it attacks the immune system** by infecting white blood cells, therefore, the defences that are needed in order to fight the virus do not work properly.
- **it mutates in the body** so even if a vaccine was developed, the virus can mutate rapidly and produce new strains which are not affected by the antibodies being produced by the body.

Choices

Individuals have the right to say no to a vaccination. However, the more unvaccinated individuals there are in a population, the greater the chance of an outbreak of the disease and the faster it will spread.

HT In order to prevent an epidemic of a disease like measles in a population, it is important that as many individuals as possible are vaccinated.

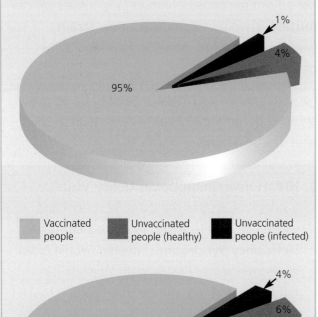

1%
4%
95%

Vaccinated people | Unvaccinated people (healthy) | Unvaccinated people (infected)

4%
6%
90%

If over 95% of the population are vaccinated then the unvaccinated will be protected too. This is because the risk of coming into contact with an infected person is very small.

If the percentage drops below 95%, unvaccinated individuals are more likely to come into contact with infected people and will pass the disease onto others who are unvaccinated (often members of the same family).

Vaccination Policy

Health authorities have to develop a policy (plan of action) for each different vaccination, which will benefit a majority of people. However, because people hold different views, there will always be some who disagree with the policy.

HT Here are some of the key factors that must be considered when trying to decide on the best course of action:

- **How high is the risk of infection?**
  Some diseases like German measles are common in the UK, whilst others like typhoid are not such a risk.
- **Who is most at risk?**
  The very young, the elderly and people living in poverty (poor diet, etc.) might be at higher risk.
- **Is the vaccination safe?**
  The vaccination needs to have been fully tested to ensure it is effective and has no adverse effects.
- **What is the cost?**
  Can the Government afford to offer a free vaccine to everyone who needs one? Would the money be better spent elsewhere?

There is always a difference between what **can** be done and what **should** be done (see p.9)

For example, the government might have the ability to vaccinate everyone in the country, but it would be unacceptable to force everyone to have the vaccination. Here are just a few reasons why:

- we live in a free society and have the right to choose for ourselves
- vaccination may conflict with the religious / personal beliefs of an individual
- some individuals may be more susceptible to the potential side effects than others.

Different courses of action may be taken in different social and environmental contexts (see p.9).

Antibiotics

Bacteria and fungi can be killed by chemicals (or drugs) called **antibiotics**. Viruses cannot be killed by antibiotics. This is why doctors do not prescribe them for colds and flu.

Resistance to Antibiotics

Over a period of time, bacteria and fungi can become **resistant** to antibiotics.

> **HT** Random mutations can occur in the genes of microorganisms, which lead to new strains developing. Some of these new strains of bacteria and fungi are less affected by the antibiotics previously used so they are able to reproduce and pass on the resistance.

As more and more varieties of bacteria and fungi become resistant to certain types of antibiotics, there are fewer ways of defeating them.

There is growing concern that microorganisms which are resistant to *all* types of drugs will eventually develop. These are what the media dub **superbugs**.

In the UK, there are already diseases such as MRSA (Methicillin Resistant *Staphylococcus aureus*), drug-resistant TB and *Clostridium difficile* (an infection of the intestines), which have a high degree of drug resistance.

To help prevent resistance to antibiotics increasing…
- doctors should only prescribe them when completely necessary
- patients should always complete a course of antibiotics, even if they are feeling better.

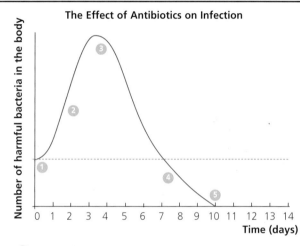

The Effect of Antibiotics on Infection

Number of harmful bacteria in the body vs *Time (days)*

1. Harmful bacteria enter the body (by food poisoning).
2. Bacteria multiply. Patient begins to feel unwell.
3. Patient visits doctor. Starts taking antibiotics.
4. Number of bacteria now lower than originally entered the body. Patient feels better (but bacteria not all dead).
5. All harmful bacteria now destroyed.

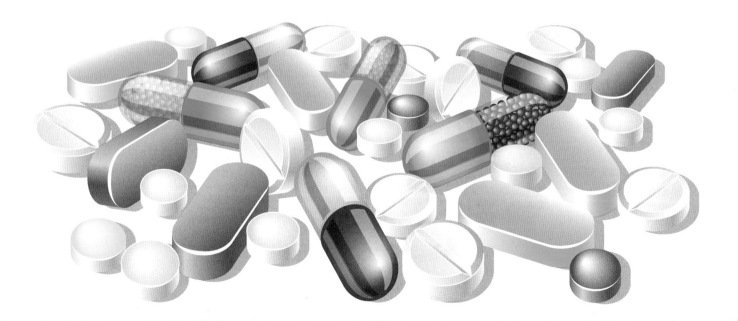

Keeping Healthy

Testing New Drugs

Scientists are always trying to develop new drugs to fight infection. Before they can be used, it is essential that the drugs are tested for **safety** and **effectiveness**. The methods used for testing drugs are often controversial.

Tests on different types of human cells grown in the laboratory

Advantages

- Shows if drugs are effective at fighting microorganisms.
- Shows if drugs will cause damage to cells.
- No people or animals are harmed.

Disadvantages

- Does not show effects of drugs on whole organism.
- Some people believe that growing human cells in this way is unnatural or wrong.

Tests on animals

Advantages

- Shows if drugs are effective within body conditions.
- Shows if drugs are safe for whole body.

Disadvantages

- Animals can suffer and die as a result of the tests.
- Animals might react differently to humans.

Following these initial tests (which can take years) **clinical trials** are carried out on **healthy volunteers** to test for **safety**, and on people with the **illness** to test for **safety** and **effectiveness**.

Clinical trials normally compare the effects of the new drugs to old ones. They have to be carefully planned to ensure the results are as accurate and reliable as possible. There are two types of trial:

1 Blind Trials

The patient does not know which drugs they are being given but the doctor does. If the patient knows what drug they had been given, they might give biased information. However, it is possible that the doctor's body language or reactions might give away information.

2 Double-blind Trials

Neither the patient nor the doctor knows which drug is being used. This means the results should be very accurate, removing bias. Although this is preferable, sometimes it is impossible to keep this information from the doctor, e.g. if the new drug has a different taste or different effects on the body.

Placebos (dummy drugs containing no medication) are occasionally used in clinical trials. However, this is not common practice because they create an **ethical** dilemma:

Trials involving placebos benefit society, because they help to establish whether a new drug is effective or not.

However, when doctors give sick patients a placebo they are offering them false hope; the patient hopes the pill will cure them, but the doctor knows it will not.

It is also difficult to disguise a placebo. If a new drug is expected to produce certain side effects and the patient does not display them, they may deduce that a placebo has been given.

For example, if a diuretic (increases urine production) is being tested, it would be easy to tell if the patient had been given the actual drug rather than a placebo.

The Heart

All living cells use oxygen to release energy from glucose. This process is called **respiration**.

The heart pumps blood around the body to provide the cells with oxygen (from the lungs) and nutrients, and take away waste materials.

The heart itself is made up of muscle cells. This means that it also needs a blood supply to keep functioning.

Arteries and Veins

The main blood vessels for transporting blood are **arteries** and **veins**. Their structure is related to their function.

Arteries carry blood away from the heart **towards** the organs. Substances from the blood cannot pass through the artery walls.

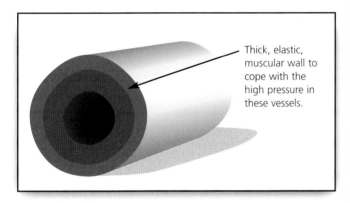

Thick, elastic, muscular wall to cope with the high pressure in these vessels.

Veins carry blood from the organs **back** to the heart. Substances cannot pass through the veins' walls.

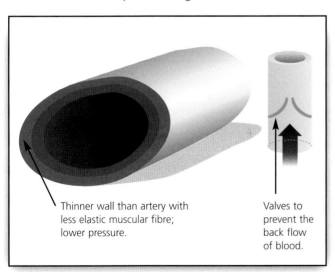

Thinner wall than artery with less elastic muscular fibre; lower pressure.

Valves to prevent the back flow of blood.

Heart Disease

Heart disease is a structural or functional abnormality of the heart, which can lead to a heart attack. It is usually caused by **lifestyle** and / or **genetic factors** not by infection (i.e. microorganisms). Elements of lifestyle that can lead to heart disease include…

- excessive alcohol intake
- poor diet
- smoking
- stress.

Fatty deposits can build up in the blood vessels supplying the heart. This means that blood flow is restricted and the muscle cells do not get the oxygen and nutrients that they need. This can cause a **heart attack**.

In the UK heart disease is much more common than in non-industrialised countries like Cambodia or Rwanda. This is probably because people in the UK are less active, e.g. they drive everywhere and use machines to do work, and the typical diet in the UK is high in salt and fats.

Reducing the Risk

There are precautions people can take to reduce the risk of heart disease.

- Exercise regularly (aim to raise the heart rate, without putting it under too much stress) e.g. 20 minutes of brisk walking every day.
- Do not smoke.
- Maintain a healthy body weight.
- Reduce salt intake, e.g. avoid salty foods and do not add salt to food.
- Monitor cholesterol levels (and use cholesterol reducing foods / drugs if necessary).

Keeping Healthy

Epidemiological Studies

If we can identify which lifestyle factors lead to heart disease, we can take action to prevent it.

Scientists try to identify these factors by examining the **incidence** (number of cases) and **distribution** of heart disease in large populations. These investigations are called **epidemiological studies**.

Correlation

Scientists look at a large **sample** (lots of individual cases, which represent a cross-section of the population) to see if there is a **correlation** (link) between a particular **factor** and an **outcome** like heart disease.

One correlation that has already been identified is between a high-fat diet (factor) and heart attacks (outcome). That is to say, a large proportion of people who suffered heart attacks had a high-fat diet.

It is important to remember that not all people who ate a fatty diet had a heart attack. This suggests that a fatty diet increases the chance of having a heart attack, but does not **always** lead to one.

> **HT** A correlation between a factor and an outcome does not necessarily mean that the factor is a cause.
>
> For example, a fictional study of obesity could uncover a positive correlation between the number of cans of diet cola an individual drinks and the number of kilograms they are overweight. This does not mean that diet cola **causes** people to be overweight. There is an alternative explanation – these people might drink diet cola **because** they are overweight!

Samples

Scientists have to look at a large sample to produce reliable results and establish what is typical and what is atypical (unusual) in a population.

An individual case might be atypical. However, without comparing it to lots of other cases, you would not know this and could easily reach the wrong conclusion.

For example, an individual who has smoked for most of his life might live to 98 without getting heart disease or lung cancer. If you looked at this case alone you might think that smoking helps you live longer!

To ensure a **fair test**, the individuals in a sample should be closely matched so that only the factor being investigated varies.

For example, if you were investigating the effect of smoking on life expectancy, the individuals in the sample would all need to have a similar diet and alcohol intake to ensure that those factors didn't affect the results.

> **HT** Data gathered through investigations can be used to argue whether or not a particular factor increases the chance of an outcome and make predictions, for example look at the graph below.
>
>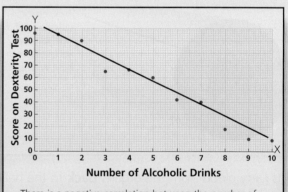
>
> There is a negative correlation between the number of alcoholic drinks consumed and a person's dexterity (ability to move hands easily). As X increases, Y decreases. This means that given a value for X it is possible to make a prediction of the value of Y.

Even if a correlation between a factor and an outcome is supported by data, scientists might still reject it.

It is only likely to be accepted if scientists can find a plausible (likely) explanation for how that factor can bring about the outcome, based on what they already know about how the body works.

The Peer Review Process

Scientists follow procedures when conducting scientific research, like epidemiological studies, to ensure their findings are reliable:

1 Epidemiological Study

The scientist discovers a correlation between a factor and an outcome and makes a hypothesis, e.g. that factor X increases the chance of outcome Y.

2 Further Investigation

The scientist conducts further experiments / observational studies to gather data to test the hypothesis.

3 Reports Findings

The scientist writes a paper detailing the hypothesis, how the experiment was carried out, the results, and the conclusion (whether the data gathered supports the hypothesis or not).

4 Peer Review

The paper is sent out to the scientist's **peers** (other scientists who work in that field). They check and evaluate the paper to see if there are any faults or flaws. They may even repeat the experiments to see if they get the same results.

5 Findings Released

If it is decided that the research was carried out correctly and the conclusions are accurate, then the findings are published in a science journal or presented at a seminar.

6 Feedback

Once the findings have been released, all scientists can evaluate the evidence for themselves. The information might lead to further advances by other scientists. It could also be challenged – particularly if someone spots a problem that the initial reviewers (see stage 4) did not identify.

This process is very important. The more scientists that review and evaluate the findings, the more likely it is that errors and potential problems will be spotted, and the more reliable the results are likely to be.

Sometimes **preliminary results** (results that have not been fully reviewed by other scientists) are leaked to the press.

These results are not reliable and may turn out to be inaccurate or wrong. If the public are given inaccurate information like this it can cause problems, e.g. it can cause false hope or panic.

HT Unfortunately there are a small minority of scientists who make claims that are not true. They might do this to improve their reputation or to get more money / funding.

If a new scientific claim is reliable, other scientists should be able to conduct the same experiment and get the same results. If this is not possible, the scientific community **will not** trust the claim.

Likewise, if a scientist refuses to hand over evidence to support their claim (e.g. details of the experiments conducted and data collected) then their findings must be taken as being unreliable.

Monthly Scientist   April 2007

Faked Data, Misconduct and Lies

The work of a top Korean scientist came under the microscope this month, when an investigation revealed that his 'ground breaking' stem cell research was underpinned by a series of fabrications and lies.

The scandal highlights the need for an international regulatory body.

The role of such a body would be to preserve the integrity of the scientific community by implementing a compulsory review process to verify claims before they are released into the public domain…

Keeping Healthy – Summary

Science Explanations

Maintenance of Life

- All living cells respire.
- The heart pumps blood around the body, transporting oxygen from the lungs to the cells.
- The risk of heart disease is increased by poor diet, stress, smoking and excessive drinking of alcohol, and can be reduced by regular, moderate exercise.

The Germ Theory of Disease

- Many diseases are caused by microorganisms (e.g. bacteria, fungi and viruses) which are all around us.
- The body has natural barriers against microorganisms: the skin, chemicals in tears and sweat, and stomach acid.
- Conditions in the body mean that when microorganisms get in they reproduce very quickly.
- The symptoms of disease are caused by the microorganisms damaging cells or releasing toxins.
- The body's immune system fights against infections: some white blood cells engulf microorganisms and digest them, whilst others produce antibodies to destroy them.
- Different microorganisms require different antibodies.
- A vaccine is a modified microorganism (incapable of causing disease), which is injected into the body. The body produces antibodies, which means that it can produce them again rapidly if needed.

> **HT**
> - Vaccines are less effective against viruses because they can mutate and produce new strains.
> - It is difficult to develop a vaccine against HIV because the virus has a high mutation rate within the body.

- Microorganisms can cause illness, and even death, if the body does not destroy them quickly enough.
- Bacteria and fungi (not viruses) can be killed by chemicals called antibiotics.
- Over time bacteria and fungi can become resistant to antibiotics.

> **HT**
> - Mutations in the genes of bacteria and fungi can result in strains that are resistant to antibiotics.

- It is important to only use antibiotics when necessary and to complete the prescribed course.

Ideas about Science

Correlation and Cause

- There is a correlation between a factor and an outcome if…
  - the outcome always / often, or never / infrequently occurs when the factor is present
  - the outcome never / infrequently, or always / often occurs when the factor is not present.

> **HT**
> - A correlation between a factor and an outcome does not always mean that one causes the other.

The Scientific Community

- Scientific findings are only accepted once they have been checked and evaluated by other scientists.
- For scientists to accept a claim there needs to be a plausible explanation as to how a factor can bring about an outcome.
- If evidence is reliable other scientists should be able to repeat the experiment with similar results.

Decisions about Science

- Some scientific practices have ethical implications. There are often lots of different views and people disagree about what is right and what is wrong.
- When developing a policy concerning a scientific practice, like vaccination, it is important to look at what *can* be done and what *should* be done.
- Because different societies have different views and different resources available, they are likely to arrive at different decisions regarding scientific practices, like vaccination.

Module B3

We are continually searching for an answer to the question of how life on Earth began and how different species evolved. This module looks at...

- how life on Earth began
- how creatures have evolved over time
- evolution by natural selection
- selective breeding
- nervous and communication systems.

Life on Earth

Life on Earth began about 3500 million years ago, and during that time there has been a large number of species living on the Earth. A species is a group of organisms which can freely breed with each other to produce fertile offspring.

We know that the very first living things developed from simple molecules that could copy or replicate themselves. However, it is not known whether the molecules were produced by conditions on Earth at the time (due to harsh surface conditions, or in deep sea vents) or whether the molecules arrived on Earth from an external source, e.g. a comet hitting the Earth.

There have been experiments that simulated the harsh conditions on Earth millions of years ago, which have led to simple organic molecules developing. There is also evidence of simple organic molecules existing in gas clouds in space and in comets.

Timescale of the Earth

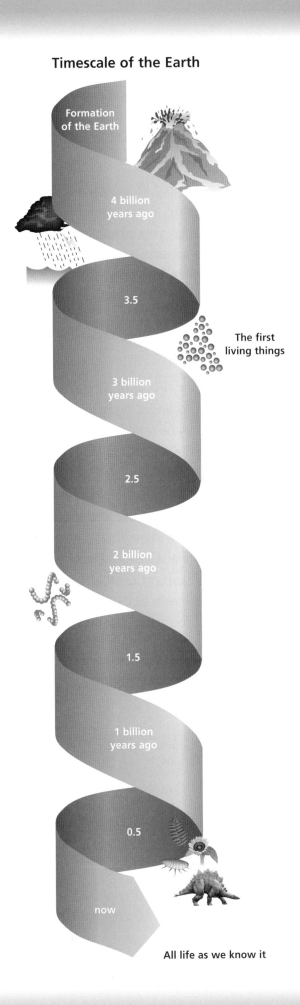

Formation of the Earth

4 billion years ago

3.5

The first living things

3 billion years ago

2.5

2 billion years ago

1.5

1 billion years ago

0.5

now

All life as we know it

Life on Earth

The Beginning of Life

Whilst scientists are still investigating how life began on Earth, there is evidence to suggest that all existing organisms share certain traits, including cellular structure and genetic code.

This would mean that all existing organisms share a **common ancestor**, and have evolved from very simple living things, which had already developed the most fundamental cellular process. There are two sources of evidence to support this hypothesis.

1 The Fossil Record

Fossils are the remains of plants or animals from many years ago which are found in rock.

Fossils indicate the history of species and can show the evolutionary changes in organisms over millions of years. They can be formed...

- from the hard parts of animals that do not decay easily
- from parts of animals and plants which have not decayed because one or more of the conditions needed for decay were absent, e.g. oxygen, moisture, temperature or correct pH levels
- from the soft parts of organisms which can be replaced by minerals as they decay. This can preserve the traces of footprints, burrows or rootlets.

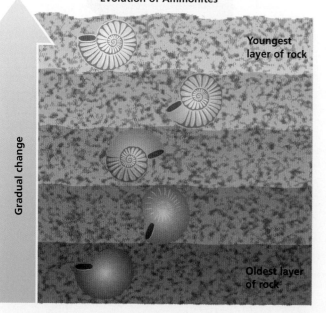

Evolution of Ammonites

Youngest layer of rock

Gradual change

Oldest layer of rock

2 DNA Evidence

Not every dead organism has been preserved as a fossil. However, analysing the DNA of both living organisms and fossilised specimens shows similarities and differences, and this can be used to fill in gaps that exist in the fossil record. The more shared genes that organisms have, the more closely related they are.

Comparing the gene sequences of organisms reveals that some organisms have a high degree of similarity in their DNA even with organisms that they are less obviously related to.

For example, human DNA sequences share 98.8% of a chimpanzee's DNA. The chimpanzee is our nearest genetic relative. A mouse, on the other hand, which appears very dissimilar from humans, shares 85% of a chimpanzee's DNA.

Mouse   Chimpanzee   Human

In whatever way life initially started, it is only through **evolution by natural selection** that life on the planet is as it is today. If the conditions on Earth had been different, at any time, to what they actually were, then evolution by natural selection could have produced very different results.

Evolution by Natural Selection

Evolution is the slow, continual change in a population over a large number of generations. It may result in the formation of a new species, the members of which are better adapted to their environment.

Evolution occurs due to **natural selection**. This is where individuals in a population have certain characteristics which improve their chances of survival in their physical environment. They are, therefore, more likely to live to adulthood and reproduce, passing on their favourable characteristics to their offspring. Individuals with poorly fitting characteristics are less likely to survive and reproduce.

So the number of individuals with the favourable traits increases whilst the number of those with unfavourable traits decreases.

There are four key points to remember in terms of natural selection:

1. Individuals within a population show **variation**, i.e. differences due to their genes.

2. There is **competition** between individuals for food and mates, etc. Also predation and disease keeps population sizes constant in spite of the production of many offspring.

3. Individuals which are **better adapted** to the environment are more likely to survive, breed successfully and produce offspring. This is termed **survival of the fittest**.

4. These survivors will **pass on their genes** to their offspring resulting in the evolution of an improved organism over generations.

Natural selection relies on variation. Variation in individuals is caused by the **environment** and **genes**.

However, *only* a genetic variation can be passed on. For example, if you had an accident and lost one of your fingers, this new characteristic would not be passed on to your offspring; this is an example of **environmental variation**.

Peppered Moths are naturally pale and speckled in colour. This means they are well camouflaged against the bark of silver birch trees.

However, during the Industrial Revolution, air pollution from the factories and mills discoloured the bark of the trees with soot and natural selection led to a new variety of Peppered moth.

1. **Variation** – Some Peppered Moths, about 10%, were naturally darker than others due to their genes.

2. **Competition** – The darker-coloured moths and paler moths had to compete for food and water.

3. **Better adapted** – The darker moths were better camouflaged against the blackened bark of trees and soot on buildings. The paler moths were much more easily seen by birds and were therefore eaten.

4. **Passing on genes** – The darker moths were more likely to survive and breed, passing on their blacker genes.

In the mid-1950s the Government passed the Clean Air Act. This dramatically reduced air pollution and so more silver birch trees stayed 'silver'. This meant that the pale variety (now about 10% of population) had an advantage and so, due to natural selection, began to grow again in numbers. Today, the presence of the pale variety of Peppered Moth is regarded as a marker for clean air.

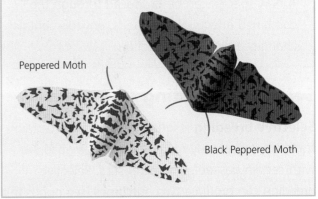

Peppered Moth

Black Peppered Moth

Life on Earth

Gene Mutation

When a change occurs in a gene it is called a **mutation**.

Mutations take place in DNA. Most of the time the mutations are corrected. However, occasionally a mutation can take place that alters the properties of a protein and can influence the development of an organism.

If this happens in a sex cell then the mutated gene can be passed on to the offspring, which may show new characteristics.

Example of a Gene Mutation

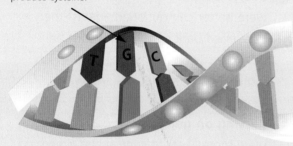

These three bases produce cysteine.

This base has mutated so now the amino acid tyrosine is produced.

A new species can be produced through the combined effects of mutations, environmental changes and natural selection.

Selective Breeding

Selective breeding is where animals with certain traits are deliberately mated to produce offspring with certain desirable characteristics. Selective breeding can produce two outcomes (see opposite):

1 Creating New Varieties of Organism

Dalmatian dogs

Choose the spottiest two to breed...

... and then the spottiest of their offspring...

... to eventually get Dalmatians.

2 Increasing the Yields of Animals and Plants

Some breeds of cattle have been bred to produce high yields of milk or milk with a high fat content.

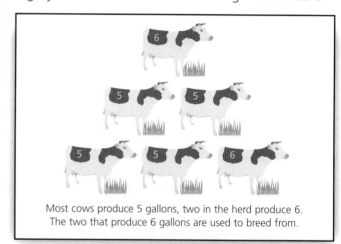

Most cows produce 5 gallons, two in the herd produce 6. The two that produce 6 gallons are used to breed from.

Improved crops can be obtained by selective breeding programmes, although this happens over a very long period of time.

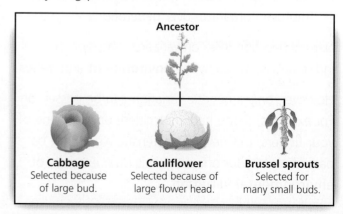

Ancestor

Cabbage
Selected because of large bud.

Cauliflower
Selected because of large flower head.

Brussel sprouts
Selected for many small buds.

The Evolution of Humans

The similarities between great apes and humans have been obvious to mankind for some time, and it is thought that they shared a **common ancestor**. Although the fossil records for human ancestors is sparse, it was through the investigation of the fossilised remains that scientists built up a human family tree showing human evolution.

A **Hominid** is any member of the biological family Hominidea (the 'great apes') including humans, gorillas and orang-utans. During evolution, the hominid family diverged (branched) and several Homo species (Homo being Latin for 'person') developed.

In modern classification, *Homo sapiens* is the *only* living species of its type. There were other Homo species, all of which are now extinct. While some of these other species might have been ancestors of Homo sapiens, it is likely that others were '**cousins**', who evolved away from our ancestral line.

Members of the Homo group include…
- *Homo habilis* – evidence exists that they were the earliest ancestor. They made and used simple tools from stone and animal bone.
- *Homo erectus* – had large brains and may have used fire to cook their food.
- *Homo sapiens* – humans today.
- *Homo neanderthalensis* – a close cousin of *Homo sapiens*.

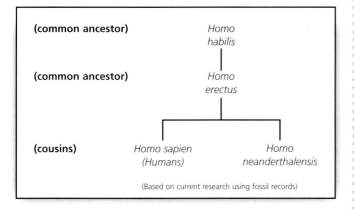

(common ancestor)	Homo habilis	
(common ancestor)	Homo erectus	
(cousins)	Homo sapien (Humans)	Homo neanderthalensis

(Based on current research using fossil records)

Over a period of 300 million years, the brain size of hominids increased. This is likely to be due to natural selection, as there is a rough correlation

between brain size and intelligence. Individuals with larger brains would have had a greater intellectual capacity (ability to process information from the environment). This would give them an advantage over those with smaller brains, making them more likely to survive and pass on their genes onto their offspring.

Based on this correlation, it was initially thought that brain size would have increased first and then hominids would have learned to walk upright. However, fossil evidence suggests that walking upright came first.

This shows how important new observations and data are in helping to establish the reliability of an explanation and improve our scientific understanding.

If new observations or data agree with a theory it increases confidence in the explanation.

> **HT** However, it does not necessarily prove that the theory is correct.

If new observations or data disagree with a theory, it indicates that either the observations or data are wrong, or the theory is wrong.

> **HT** This, therefore, may decrease our confidence in the explanation.

In the latter situation, further investigations are carried out to establish where the error lies. If the new observations or data prove to be reliable, then the existing theory will be revised or changed. This is how scientific explanations change and develop over time.

Life on Earth

Origins of Life

How life on Earth began is a question that has been debated by different religions and scientists for years.

In general terms, religions believe that God, or a creator, created all life. Scientists, on the other hand, noted how organisms looked similar to each other, and over the years have developed testable theories to try to explain these similarities.

Theory of Inheritance of Acquired Characteristics

Jean-Baptiste Lamarck believed that an animal evolved within its lifetime. He put forward the hypothesis that the more an animal used a part of its body, the more likely it would be that it would adapt to be better at that job. For example, a giraffe stretching for leaves on a tall tree would develop a long neck, a characteristic which would then be passed onto its offspring.

Then later, Weismann, a scientist, experimented on mice. He cut their tails off and then bred them. However, he found that the tail-less mice produced offspring with tails. This new data conflicted with Lamarck's explanation and cast doubt on his theory. Lamarck countered this by saying that experiments like Weismann's did not count because it was a deliberate mutation; only those situations where the animal itself desired a change were valid. However, this new evidence led to Lamarck's theory being rejected.

Lamarck is an example of a scientist using imagination and creativity to develop an explanation.

HT A scientific explanation is not abandoned as soon as new data is found that conflicts with it for a number of reasons:

- the new data may be incorrect
- explanations based on new data have the potential to run into problems quickly
- lots of scientists will have based work on the existing explanation and will be inclined to stick with what has served them well in the past.

Therefore, a new explanation is only likely to replace it when it has been tried and tested, and proven to be reliable.

Evolution by Natural Selection

In the 1830s, Charles Darwin consolidated existing ideas about evolution and created a testable theory of how evolution takes place. His work was based on observable evidence, e.g. studies of the different types of finch on the Galapagos Islands. By collecting data, Darwin made four important observations which were at the heart of his theory of evolution: variety, competition, survival of the fittest, and passing on desirable characteristics to the next generation (see p.25)

HT Darwin **linked these observations** and deduced that all organisms were involved in a struggle for survival in which only the best-adapted organisms would be able to survive, reproduce and pass on their characteristics. This formed the basis for his famous theory of 'Evolution by Natural Selection'.

There are many different theories and scientists cannot be absolutely certain about how life on Earth began; it is difficult to find evidence to prove any theory, and theories are based on the best evidence at the time. No one experienced the beginning of life on Earth so it is impossible to ever be certain how it began. Even today we are making new discoveries and developing our scientific knowledge.

The Extinction of Species

Throughout the history of Earth, species of animals and plants have become **extinct** (they no longer exist anywhere on the planet), e.g. the Dodo.

The usual cause of extinction is a species' inability to adapt to change in the form of…

- increased competition
- new predators
- change in the environment
- new diseases.

There have been at least five **mass extinctions** in the history of life on Earth in which many species have disappeared in a relatively short period of geological time.

These extinctions have taken place in the last 0.5 billion years. Mass extinction occurs when a change to the environment happens so quickly, that animals and plants are not able to produce individuals able to cope with the change. For example, it is thought that the dinosaurs were killed when an asteroid hit the Earth, which would have caused dramatic and immediate environmental changes.

Human activity, whether directly or indirectly, has been responsible for the extinction of some species. Such human activity includes:

- The introduction of new predators or competition to areas where the animal or plant previously had no natural competitors or predators, e.g. the Mitten crab travelled in ballast tanks of ships from Asia to the UK. The crab eats native species of crab.
- Industrial activities increase the amount of greenhouse gases in the atmosphere, which are responsible for global warming.

- Deforestation clears whole habitats, increases the amount of carbon dioxide in the atmosphere and alters the carbon cycle.

If unchecked, these changes can and will cause species to become extinct.

Example:

Extinctions Caused Directly by Man:
The **Great Auk**. This sea bird lived in places like Canada, Iceland and Britain. They were hunted for food and their down was used for mattresses. The last pair of Great Auks was killed by hunters on July 3rd 1844. The auk only laid one egg a year and could not fly to escape, so was vulnerable to hunters.
Smallpox. This virus was declared eradicated (extinct) in 1980 by the World Health Organisation. The only examples of the virus are currently stored in two laboratories, one in America, the other in Russia. The virus was eradicated deliberately by man by mass vaccination (intentionally removing the habitat of the virus).

Extinctions Caused Indirectly by Man:
The **Rodrigues pigeon**. This bird was native to the Rodrigues Island in the Indian Ocean. It became extinct when ships visiting the island accidentally introduced rats, which preyed on the birds.
The **Gould's Mouse**. This Australian animal, slightly smaller than a rat, disappeared rapidly after settlement by Europeans in the 1840s. They were thought to have been brought to extinction due to being hunted by cats, and killed by diseases from rats and mice (all introduced by man). They were also affected by changes to their habitat.

Life on Earth

Maintaining Biodiversity

Every time a species becomes extinct, information stored in the organisms' genetic code is lost. There are now projects to prevent this, like the Kew Gardens Millennium Seed Bank Project, which aims to safeguard 24 000 plant species from around the globe against extinction. This is achieved by collecting and storing seeds from all over the world.

Extinctions mean less variety on Earth. Without this variety people would start to run out of food crops and medicines. Many medicines are developed from plants and animals, for example the foxglove was found to contain a chemical, digitalis, that could be used to treat heart disease.

There are potentially an unknown number of medicines existing in the genetic code of animals and plants living in areas such as the Amazon rainforest – an area which is losing 25 000 square kilometres a year to deforestation. By understanding how our actions can impact on biodiversity, scientists hope to discover ways to use the Earth's resources in a **sustainable** way, so that future generations can enjoy a similar diversity of living things.

Food Chains

Organisms do not live in isolation from one another. There is competition for resources between different species of animals or plants in the same habitat. Food chains can be used to show the direction of energy and material transfer between organisms, and which organisms are eating other organisms.

Example

Energy from the Sun enters the food chain when green plants absorb sunlight in order to photosynthesise. When animals eat the plants the energy passes from one organism to another up the food chain.

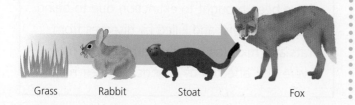

Grass   Rabbit   Stoat   Fox

The animals are all dependent upon each other and their environment. For example, if all the rabbits became extinct, then the stoat would be at risk of starving, which, in turn, would put the fox at risk. In reality, most animals are not just dependent upon one food source, so the stoats and foxes would not all die, but their numbers would probably be reduced, as competition for the remaining food sources would increase.

Food Webs

Food webs are drawn to show how all the food chains in a given habitat are inter-related. In practice these can be very complicated because many animals have varied diets.

Food Web

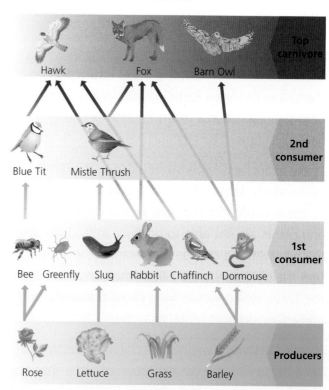

Changes to the environment can alter numbers in the food web. For example, a small change in the amount of rain could reduce the amount of lettuces and cause reductions in numbers of slugs. If the changes are too great for the natural variation within a population to accommodate, then organisms will die out before they can reproduce. The population will decline and eventually become extinct.

Nervous and Communication Systems

The evolution of multi-cellular organisms eventually led to specialised cells working together as tissue. Different tissues working together formed organs, and collections of organs working together formed organ systems.

This led to the development of **nervous** and **hormonal** communication systems. There are several differences between the messages in the two systems:

Nerve Impulses
- Electrical impulses in nerves
- Rapid action
- Last a short time.

Hormone Signals
- Chemical messages in blood
- Slow action
- Last a long time.

> The maintenance of a constant internal body environment (temperature, water balance, etc.) is called **homeostasis**.
>
> The human body uses both nervous signals and hormonal signals to ensure that body systems remain stable.

Hormone Communication

Many processes within the body are coordinated by hormones. These are chemical substances, produced by glands, which are transported around the body by the bloodstream. Hormones regulate the functions of many organs and cells.

Control of **hormones** is far slower and comparatively longer-lasting than nervous impulses, because the hormones travel to the relevant effector in the bloodstream. It takes approximately 10 seconds for blood to travel once around the body.

Example 1: Human Fertility
A woman naturally produces hormones that cause the maturation and release of an egg from her ovaries, and also cause changes in the thickness of the lining of her womb. The hormones are produced by the pituitary gland and the ovaries.

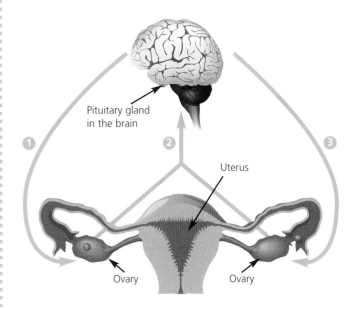

1. Follicle stimulating hormone (FSH) from the pituitary gland causes the ovaries to produce oestrogen and an egg to mature.
2. Oestrogen, produced in the ovaries, inhibits the production of FSH and causes the production of luteinising hormone (LH).
3. LH, also from the pituitary gland, stimulates the release of an egg in the middle of the menstrual cycle.

Example 2: Insulin
Insulin is a hormone produced by the pancreas; its level in the blood is governed by the amount of glucose in the blood. If the concentration of glucose increases, insulin is then released into the bloodstream.

The presence of insulin causes cells (which need glucose for respiration) to take in the glucose. Any additional glucose is then stored as glycogen. The transportation (movement) of glucose is governed by the circulatory system.

Life on Earth

The Central Nervous System

The nervous system is based around sensor (receptor) cells that detect **stimuli**, and effector cells which **respond** to the stimuli. Nerve cells (neurons) connect the sensor cells (e.g. in eyes, ears and skin) and effector cells (e.g. muscles / glands) together.

Neurons are specially adapted cells that can carry an electrical signal, e.g. a nerve impulse.

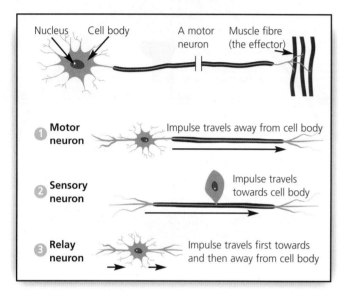

The coordination of the nervous system in humans, and other vertebrates, is carried out by the spinal cord and the brain. This is referred to as the **central nervous system**. Messages are sent via electrical impulses which allow fast, short-lived responses.

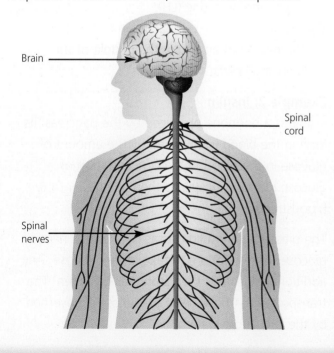

Example 1: Removing your Hand from a Pin – Involuntary Reflex Action

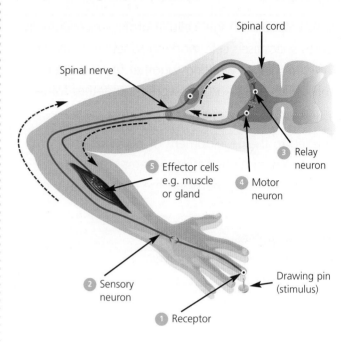

1. A receptor is stimulated by the drawing pin (stimulus)...
2. ... causing impulses to pass along a sensory neuron into the spinal cord.
3. The sensory neurone synapses (communicates) with a relay neuron, by-passing the brain.
4. The relay neuron synapses with a motor neuron, sending impulses down it...
5. ... to the muscles (effectors) causing them to contract and remove the hand in response to the sharp drawing pin.

Example 2: Turning Down Loud Music – Voluntary Reaction

Sound-sensitive receptors in the ear detect loud music.

The sensory neurons then pass an electrical signal to the central nervous system where the information is processed.

A response, in the form of another electrical signal, is sent by the motor neuron to the effector cells in the muscles in the arms and fingers.

The arm and finger muscles respond by covering the ears to try and block the sound and then turning the volume down.

Life on Earth – Summary

Science Explanations

The Interdependence of Living Things

- A food web can show which organisms eat other organisms in a particular habitat.
- Different species in a particular habitat often compete for the same space or food source.
- A change which affects one species in a food web also affects other species in the same food web.
- Ecosystems can often adjust to changes but large disruptions may change an ecosystem permanently.

Maintenance of Life

- Organisms need water, food and light to survive.
- Organisms need to avoid harmful chemicals, predators and extreme temperatures in order to survive.
- They are more likely to survive if they can sense what they need, or need to avoid, in their surroundings.
- Multi-cellular organisms have sensor cells and effector cells.
- Multi-cellular animals have nervous systems.
- Nervous systems are comprised of nerve cells (neurons) which link sensor cells to effector cells.
- In humans they are linked via the central nervous system (spinal cord and brain).
- Hormones are chemicals which travel in the blood and bring about slower, longer-lasting responses.

> **HT**
> - Nervous and hormonal communication systems are involved in maintaining a constant internal environment (homeostasis).

Theory of Evolution by Natural Selection

- The first living things developed about 3 500 million years ago from molecules that could copy themselves.
- The molecules were produced in the conditions on Earth at the time.
- Evolution occurs due to natural selection.

- If conditions on Earth had been different from what they were, natural selection could have produced very different results.
- There is variation between individuals of the same species.
- Individuals with certain characteristics have a better chance of surviving, and reproducing, if the environment changes or vital resources become scarce.
- There will be more individuals with these characteristics in the next generation, and so on.
- Selective breeding involves making deliberate selections based on desirable characteristics.
- New species have evolved over a very long period of time.

> **HT**
> - Genes can be changed by mutation.
> - Mutation can cause cancer cells.
> - Mutated genes in sex cells can be passed onto offspring and produce new characteristics.

- A large change in the environment may cause an entire species to become extinct.

> **HT**
> - A new species can be produced by the combined effects of mutations, environmental changes and natural selection.

Ideas about Science

Scientific Explanations

- For some scientific questions, there is not a definite answer yet.
- An observation that agrees with a theory increases confidence in it.
- An observation that disagrees with a theory indicates that either the observation or the theory is wrong.
- Explanations cannot simply be deduced from the available data – personal background, experience or interests may influence judgements.

Homeostasis

Homeostasis

Homeostasis is the maintenance of a constant internal environment. It is achieved by balancing bodily inputs and outputs and removing waste products.

The body has automatic control systems in place which ensure that the correct, steady levels of **temperature** and **water** are maintained.

These factors are essential in order for cells to be able to function properly.

Factors Affecting Homeostasis

Homeostasis can be affected by changes to **temperature** and **hydration levels**.

If a person is doing strenuous exercise, or lives in a very hot or cold climate, the systems in the body have to work extra hard to ensure homeostasis.

If homeostasis fails then death rapidly follows.

Exercise

When a person is doing **strenuous exercise**, the temperature inside the body increases and the body loses water through sweat. If the body cannot get rid of the excess heat then the body temperature would reach a critical level where different systems would stop working.

If the water is not replaced then vital chemical reactions would also stop. These effects, if not corrected, will lead to death.

Hot Climates

In very hot climates survival is dependent upon homeostasis. As with strenuous exercise, controlling temperature and hydration is extremely important. Body temperature can quickly escalate to critical levels and water levels can drop rapidly.

Cold Climates

In very cold climates heat is lost to the surroundings rapidly and this can lead to a condition called hypothermia. The body becomes too cold and chemical reactions stop.

HT Homeostasis can also be affected by changes in **blood oxygen levels** and **salt levels**.

If too much water is lost to the environment, then the balance of essential salts will change – their concentration will increase.

Scuba divers dive to depths where homeostasis would normally fail. Therefore, they rely on equipment to overcome these problems.

The scuba equipment controls the gases which enter the body, ensuring that dissolved oxygen is kept at the correct level.

A wetsuit traps a layer of water between the body and the inner of the suit. This layer of water warms up, insulating the body and preventing it from cooling down too much.

Mountain climbers at high altitudes have to contend with a change in air pressure. The higher up they go, the lower the air pressure becomes. This means that the amount of oxygen that can be inhaled decreases and climbers can suffer (and possibly die) from altitude sickness.

Climbers wear breathing apparatus to ensure that the correct blood oxygen level is maintained.

Artificial Homeostasis

Some individuals' homeostatic mechanisms may not work correctly and may need to be artificially supported, e.g. premature babies or patients with kidney disease.

A premature baby may not have fully functioning systems, so an **incubator** helps the baby to survive by controlling temperature and oxygen levels.

Artificial systems and body systems have similarities in that they have…

- receptors (sensors) to detect stimuli
- processing centres to receive information and coordinate responses
- effectors which produce the response automatically.

Negative Feedback

HT

The temperature inside an incubator fluctuates naturally, but it is important that the temperature is maintained within the correct range to support the life of the baby inside.

When the temperature inside the incubator exceeds a set level, it is detected by a sensor (receptor). The processing centre in the computer responds to this by sending a signal to the heater (effector) to turn the heat off. If the temperature drops below a set level it is detected by the sensor and the processing centre sends another signal to switch the heater on; this will increase the temperature. This process is an example of **negative feedback**; the receptor and effector reverse any changes to the system's steady state.

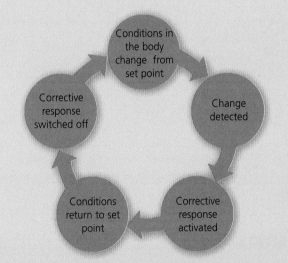

Antagonistic Effectors

In many systems there are effectors which act **antagonistically** (i.e. as opposites) to one another.

An increase in the activity of one effector is accompanied by a decrease in the activity of an antagonistic effector, e.g. one effector is responsible for increasing temperature whilst another carries out the opposite, decreasing the temperature.

This method of control is far more sensitive and accurate.

Homeostasis

Homeostasis in Cells

Homeostasis also takes place at a cellular level (i.e. inside cells). Chemical reactions taking place inside a cell need raw materials which must enter across the membrane of the cell.

Some products, including water, gases (oxygen and carbon dioxide) and other compounds, also need to be transported away from the cell.

Diffusion

Diffusion is the spontaneous and passive overall (net) movement of substances from regions where the concentration is high, to regions where the concentration is low. It is spontaneous and passive because no energy input is needed by cells to make the process work. The process is random which means that some particles can move back to where the particles are in a high concentration. However, the overall movement is from a high to low concentration.

Chemicals such as oxygen (O_2), carbon dioxide (CO_2) and dissolved food move in and out of cells by diffusion. For example, if the concentration of oxygen in a cell is low but the concentration of oxygen in the surrounding region is high, then oxygen molecules will diffuse from the surrounding region into the cell (see diagram opposite).

Osmosis

Osmosis is the diffusion of water from a dilute solution (i.e. with a high water to solute ratio) to a more concentrated solution (i.e. with a low water to solute ratio) through a partially permeable membrane.

The membrane allows the water molecules through but not solute molecules because they are too large (see Osmosis diagram ① opposite).

The effect of osmosis is to gradually dilute the concentrated solution. This is what happens at root hair cells, where water moves from the soil into the cell by osmosis, along a concentration gradient (see Osmosis diagram ② opposite).

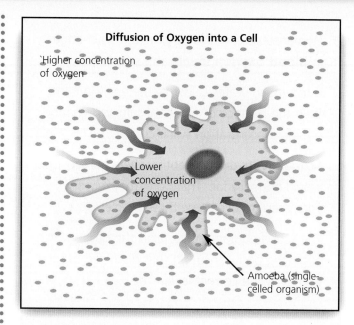

Diffusion of Oxygen into a Cell

Higher concentration of oxygen

Lower concentration of oxygen

Amoeba (single-celled organism)

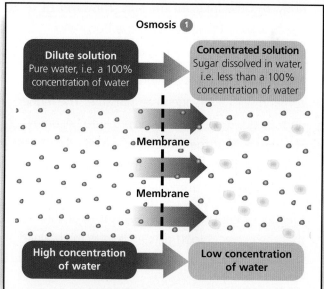

Osmosis ①

Dilute solution
Pure water, i.e. a 100% concentration of water

Concentrated solution
Sugar dissolved in water, i.e. less than a 100% concentration of water

Membrane

Membrane

High concentration of water

Low concentration of water

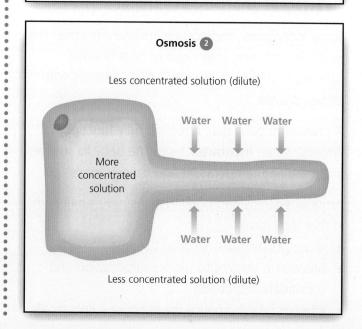

Osmosis ②

Less concentrated solution (dilute)

Water   Water   Water

More concentrated solution

Water   Water   Water

Less concentrated solution (dilute)

More on Osmosis

Animal cells, unlike plant cells, have no cell wall to support the cell membrane, so osmosis can have serious effects. There is the possibility that cells could rupture if too much water enters them. On the other hand, if a cell loses a lot of water it will be unable to carry out chemical reactions.

Animals which live in salt water (such as the sea) must conserve water because they will have a tendency to lose water through osmosis.

Animals which live in freshwater have the opposite problem – the solute concentration is greater inside their cells compared to the external water. This means that they must quickly get rid of excess water, otherwise the cells will burst.

Active Transport

Active transport is the movement of a chemical substance against a concentration gradient. This requires energy.

If a cell produces glucose then the concentration of glucose inside the cell will be higher than the concentration outside. If the glucose were able to diffuse it would leave the cell along the concentration gradient.

Cells use active transport to bring the glucose outside the cell back inside against the concentration gradient, for example in the villi in the small intestine.

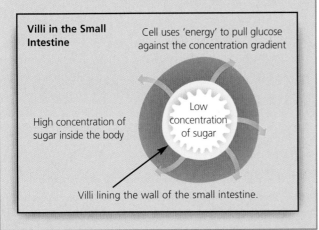

Villi in the Small Intestine

Cell uses 'energy' to pull glucose against the concentration gradient

High concentration of sugar inside the body

Low concentration of sugar

Villi lining the wall of the small intestine.

Enzymes

Enzymes are organic catalysts. They are **protein molecules** that speed up the rate of chemical reactions in living organisms. These reactions take place in cells in order to produce new materials.

Activity and Temperature

The graph below shows the effect of temperature on enzyme activity.

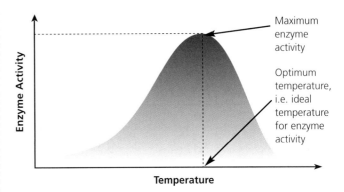

Maximum enzyme activity

Optimum temperature, i.e. ideal temperature for enzyme activity

Enzyme Activity

Temperature

At low temperatures, small increases in temperature cause an increase in the frequency and energy of collisions between reactants and enzymes, so the rate of reaction increases.

The enzyme activity increases until the **optimum temperature** is reached. After this, the increase in temperature continues to cause increased collisions, but the enzyme molecules become permanently damaged by the heat, resulting in either decreased enzyme activity, or no activity at all.

Different enzymes have different optimum working temperatures. For example, enzymes in the human body work best at about 37°C. Below this temperature the rate of reaction is **slow** whilst above 40°C the enzyme becomes **denatured**. Denaturing means the enzyme is permanently destroyed and stops working.

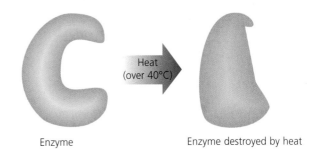

Enzyme

Heat (over 40°C)

Enzyme destroyed by heat

Homeostasis

The Lock and Key Model

Only a molecule with the correct shape can fit into an enzyme. This is a bit like a key (the molecule) fitting into a lock (the enzyme). Once the enzyme

and molecule are linked the reaction takes place, the products are released and the process is able to start again.

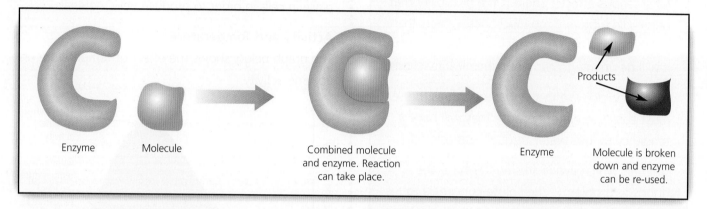

Enzyme Molecule

Combined molecule and enzyme. Reaction can take place.

Enzyme

Products

Molecule is broken down and enzyme can be re-used.

The Active Site

The place where the molecule fits is called the **active site**.

Each enzyme has a different **shape**, so it is highly specific; only certain molecules will fit into its active site.

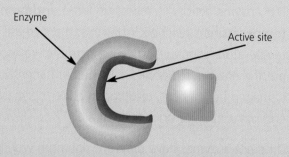

Enzyme

Active site

If an enzyme becomes denatured by being heated above a certain temperature or by being subjected to extreme pH levels, then the shape of the active site is **changed irreversibly**. This means the molecules can no longer fit and the reaction cannot take place.

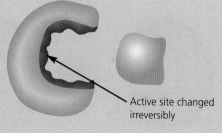

Active site changed irreversibly

The graph below shows how changes in pH levels affect enzyme activity.

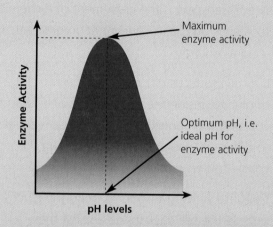

Maximum enzyme activity

Optimum pH, i.e. ideal pH for enzyme activity

Enzyme Activity

pH levels

Note that, as with temperature, there is an optimum pH level at which the enzyme works best.

As the pH level increases or decreases, the enzyme becomes less and less effective. The optimum pH of different enzymes can vary considerably.

The enzyme in human saliva works best at about pH 7.3 whilst the enzyme, pepsin, found in the stomach, needs to be in very acidic conditions in order to work well.

Maintaining Constant Body Temperature

Since enzymes work best at 37°C in humans, it is essential that the body temperature remains very close to this. In order to maintain this constant temperature, energy loss and energy gain from the body must be balanced.

The temperature of the body's extremities tends to be cooler than the core body temperature. Energy is transferred from the blood to the tissues when it reaches the cooler parts.

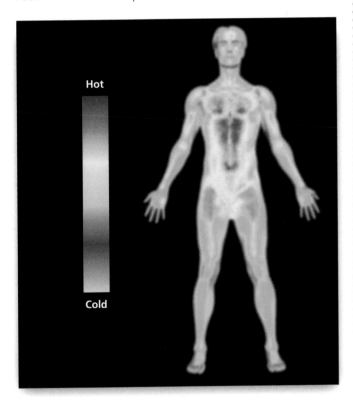

Hot

Cold

Controlling body temperature requires...
- temperature detectors in the skin to detect the external temperature
- a temperature detector in the brain to measure the temperature of the blood
- the brain, which acts as a processing centre, to receive information from the temperature receptors in the skin and in the brain
- effectors (sweat glands and muscles) which carry out the response.

The response to any change in temperature is triggered automatically.

If the temperature of the body is too high then heat needs to be transferred to the environment. This is done by sweating, since evaporation from the skin requires heat energy from the body.

If the temperature of the body is too low then the body starts to shiver. Shivering is the rapid contraction and release of muscles. These contractions require energy from increased respiration, and heat is released as a by-product, warming surrounding tissue.

Heat Stroke

Heat stroke is an uncontrolled increase in body temperature – the body cannot lose heat fast enough. A core body temperature of 40°C is life threatening. At 41°C, brain death starts to occur – the brain stops functioning properly and so cannot trigger the effectors that would normally lead to heat loss.

Increased sweating due to very hot temperatures can lead to dehydration. Dehydration stops sweating from occurring which leads to the core temperature increasing still further. If the body is not cooled down, then death will occur.

Common causes of heat stroke include exercising in very warm conditions, very high humidity, and dehydration.

Symptoms of Heat Stroke

- Confusion.
- Red / dry skin.
- Low blood pressure.
- Convulsions.
- Fainting.
- Rapid heartbeat.

Initial Treatment of Heat Stroke

- Remove clothes and bathe in cool water.
- Cool body using wet towels.
- Use a fan.
- Put ice packs on the neck, head and groin.
- Elevate (raise) legs.

Homeostasis

ⓗ Vasodilation and Vasoconstriction

Vasodilation is the widening, and vasoconstriction is the narrowing, of the blood vessels (capillaries) which run very close to the surface of the skin.

Blood temperature is monitored by a centre in the brain called the **hypothalamus**. The hypothalamus constantly monitors temperature and switches various temperature control mechanisms on and off.

In **hot conditions** blood vessels in the skin dilate causing greater heat loss – more heat is lost from the surface of the skin by radiation.

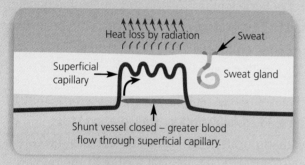

In **cold conditions** blood vessels in the skin constrict reducing heat loss – less heat is lost from the surface of the skin by radiation.

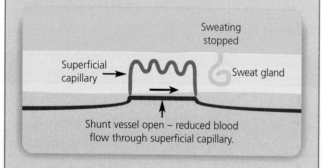

Hypothermia

Hypothermia occurs when the body is exposed to low temperatures for a long period of time. The body's heat is not replaced fast enough and, if untreated, this can lead to death.

The common cause of hypothermia is when the core body temperature falls below 35°C because it cannot get enough energy in cold conditions, and is unable to respond to the drop in body temperature.

Symptoms of Hypothermia

- Grey skin colour.
- Amnesia (memory loss).
- Shivering.
- Slurred speech.
- Confusion.
- Loss of coordination.
- Cold skin.

Initial Treatment of Hypothermia

- Raise the core body temperature.
- Insulate the body (particularly the armpits, head and groin).
- Give warm drinks, but not alcohol.
- Do not rub or massage, (this brings blood to the surface meaning even more heat is lost which can lead to heart failure).

Water Balance

Water is input (gained) from drinks, food and respiration. It is output (lost) through sweating, breathing and the excretion of faeces and urine. The body has to balance these different inputs and outputs to ensure that there is enough water inside cells for cell activity to take place.

Most people have two **kidneys**, one situated on either side of the spine on the back wall of the abdomen. It is the kidneys' job to control the balance of water in the body.

This is achieved by adjusting the amount of urine that is excreted from the body.

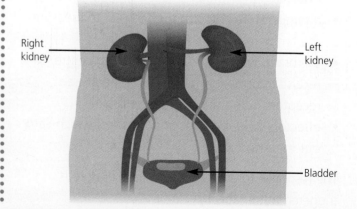

The kidneys filter the blood to remove all waste (urea) and to balance levels of other chemicals (including water). This balance is achieved by several stages:

1. Filtering small molecules from the blood to form urine (water, salt and urea).
2. Absorbing all the sugar for respiration.
3. Absorbing as much salt as the body requires.
4. Absorbing as much water as the body requires.
5. Excreting the remaining urine, which is stored in the bladder.

The brain monitors water content constantly and causes the kidneys to adjust the concentration and volume of urine produced.

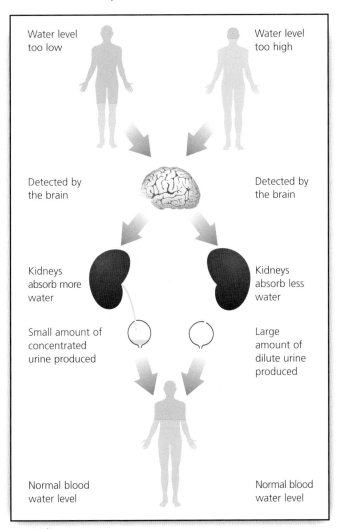

Water level too low — Water level too high

Detected by the brain — Detected by the brain

Kidneys absorb more water — Kidneys absorb less water

Small amount of concentrated urine produced — Large amount of dilute urine produced

Normal blood water level — Normal blood water level

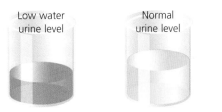

Low water urine level — Normal urine level — Excess water urine level

The amount of water that needs to be absorbed depends on a number of factors:

- **External temperature**
  If the temperature is hot then extra water will be lost as sweat. As a result, more water will need to be absorbed in the body. The urine will be a dark yellow colour with a high salt content. On colder days, less water will be lost as sweat and the urine will be a pale straw colour.

- **Amount of exercise**
  More sweat is produced during exercise, so once again the urine will be dark and will contain more dissolved salts.

- **Fluid intake**
  If not enough fluids are drunk then the urine produced will be more concentrated. Some drinks (such as coffee and tea) cause more water to be excreted. This is due to the chemical **caffeine**. Caffeine is a **diuretic** which means it increases the amount of urine produced.

  Alcohol is an even stronger diuretic than caffeine, and it causes a larger volume of more dilute urine to be produced. This then causes dehydration (one of the causes of a hangover).

- **Drugs**
  Drugs, such as Ecstasy, can interfere with the brain, causing the body to stop excreting water into the urine. A small quantity of concentrated urine is produced (whilst the blood plasma has more water than it should). If the user then drinks too much water (in response to getting hot) the water level increases in the blood. The consequence of this is that the cells rupture and, if this occurs in the brain, brain damage or death can result.

- **Salt intake**
  When salt levels increase, the body removes any excess salt by producing dilute urine. This means that more fluids need to be taken into the body to maintain a balanced water level.

Homeostasis

Urine Concentration

The concentration of urine is controlled by a hormone called anti-diuretic hormone (ADH).

ADH is released into the blood via the pituitary gland. Controlling water balance is an example of negative feedback (see diagram below).

Drugs such as alcohol and Ecstasy affect the production of ADH in different ways. Alcohol causes ADH to be suppressed and, therefore, more water leaves the body in the urine. Ecstasy causes too much ADH to be produced leading to too much water in the blood. Osmosis then causes the water to leave the blood causing brain cells to swell and burst.

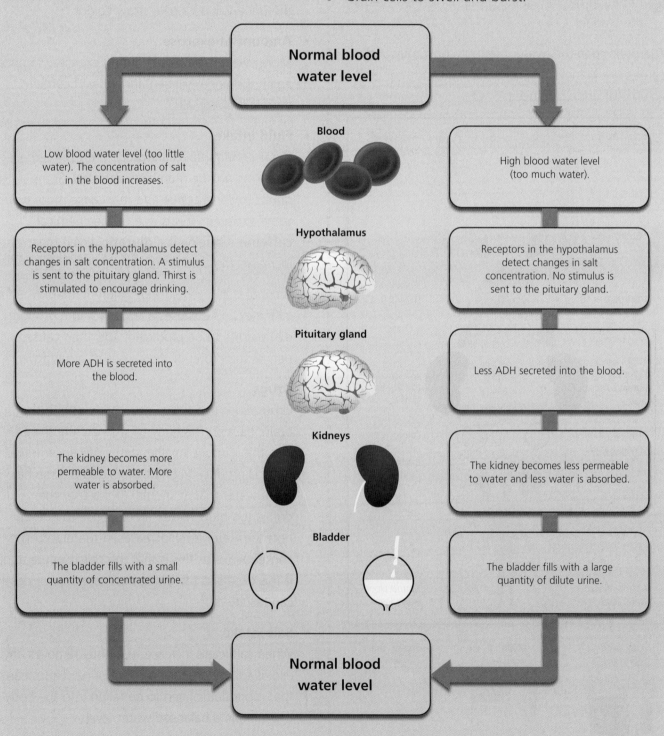

Normal blood water level

Blood

Low blood water level (too little water). The concentration of salt in the blood increases.

High blood water level (too much water).

Hypothalamus

Receptors in the hypothalamus detect changes in salt concentration. A stimulus is sent to the pituitary gland. Thirst is stimulated to encourage drinking.

Receptors in the hypothalamus detect changes in salt concentration. No stimulus is sent to the pituitary gland.

Pituitary gland

More ADH is secreted into the blood.

Less ADH secreted into the blood.

Kidneys

The kidney becomes more permeable to water. More water is absorbed.

The kidney becomes less permeable to water and less water is absorbed.

Bladder

The bladder fills with a small quantity of concentrated urine.

The bladder fills with a large quantity of dilute urine.

Normal blood water level

Module B5

Genetic technologies such as stem cell research and cellular growth control are an important part of modern medical science. This module looks at...

- how organisms produce new cells
- how genes control growth and development within the cell
- how new organisms develop from a single cell.

Cells

Cells are the building blocks of all living things. All cells contain **DNA**, which is a nucleic acid (i.e. it is found mainly in the nucleus).

DNA molecules are in the form of a double helix and contain the genetic code. DNA determines the biological development of all cellular life forms, from single-celled organisms to complex organisms.

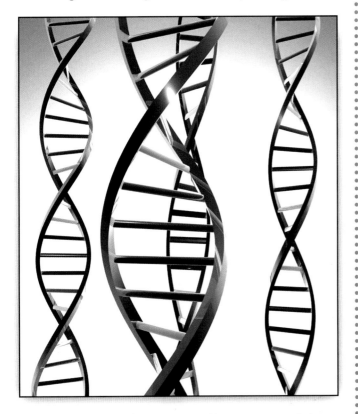

All cells contain **organelles** (different parts of the cell's structure). In general, plant and animal cells have the following structures:

Plant Cell – Palisade Cell From a Leaf

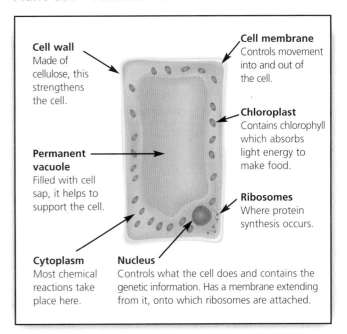

Cell wall
Made of cellulose, this strengthens the cell.

Cell membrane
Controls movement into and out of the cell.

Chloroplast
Contains chlorophyll which absorbs light energy to make food.

Permanent vacuole
Filled with cell sap, it helps to support the cell.

Ribosomes
Where protein synthesis occurs.

Cytoplasm
Most chemical reactions take place here.

Nucleus
Controls what the cell does and contains the genetic information. Has a membrane extending from it, onto which ribosomes are attached.

Animal Cell – Cheek Cell From a Human

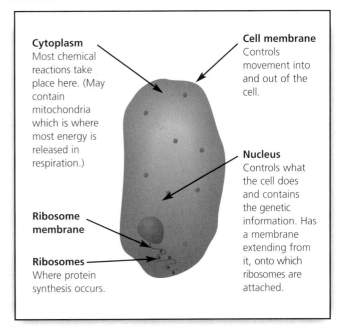

Cytoplasm
Most chemical reactions take place here. (May contain mitochondria which is where most energy is released in respiration.)

Cell membrane
Controls movement into and out of the cell.

Nucleus
Controls what the cell does and contains the genetic information. Has a membrane extending from it, onto which ribosomes are attached.

Ribosome membrane

Ribosomes
Where protein synthesis occurs.

The organelles do different jobs within the cell. For example...

- the nucleus contains the DNA
- the chloroplasts in plant cells are where photosynthesis takes place
- mitochondria are where respiration takes place
- the ribosomes interpret the coded instructions carried by DNA to make host proteins.

The organelles work together to allow the cell to perform a specific function.

Growth and Development

Mitosis

Mitosis is the process by which a cell divides to produce two new cells with identical sets of chromosomes, and the same number of chromosomes as the parent cell. They will also have all the necessary organelles. The purpose of mitosis is to produce new cells for growth and repair and to replace old tissues.

The Cell Cycle

To enable mitosis to take place, cells go through a cycle of growth and division. The cycle repeats itself until the cell can no longer divide. (In humans this is after approximately 70 cell divisions.)

Cell Growth

When a cell enters the growth phase of the cycle…

- the numbers of organelles increase
- the chromosomes are copied.

This happens because the cell is preparing to divide. Copies of all the cell's organelles and chromosomes need to be produced otherwise one daughter cell would be left incomplete and would not be able to function.

Duplicate chromosomes are produced when the two strands in each DNA molecule separate and new strands form alongside them.

Meiosis

Meiosis only takes place in the testes and ovaries. It is a special type of cell division that produces gametes (sex cells, i.e. eggs and sperm) for sexual reproduction.

Gametes contain **half** the number of chromosomes of the parent cell.

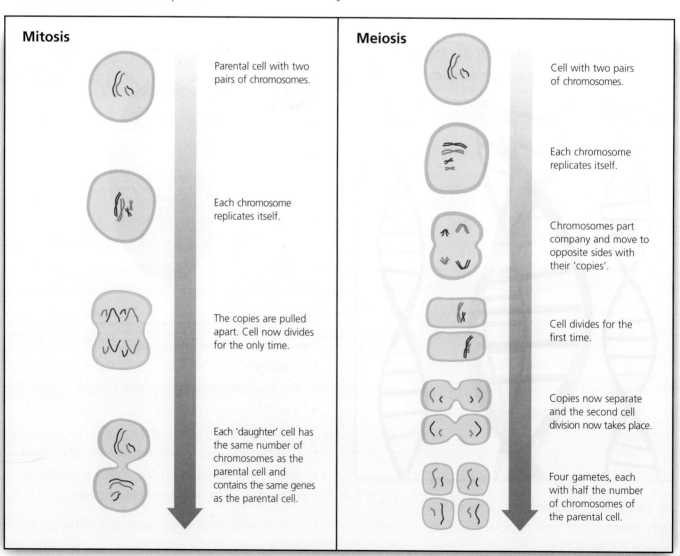

Mitosis

Parental cell with two pairs of chromosomes.

Each chromosome replicates itself.

The copies are pulled apart. Cell now divides for the only time.

Each 'daughter' cell has the same number of chromosomes as the parental cell and contains the same genes as the parental cell.

Meiosis

Cell with two pairs of chromosomes.

Each chromosome replicates itself.

Chromosomes part company and move to opposite sides with their 'copies'.

Cell divides for the first time.

Copies now separate and the second cell division now takes place.

Four gametes, each with half the number of chromosomes of the parental cell.

Fertilisation

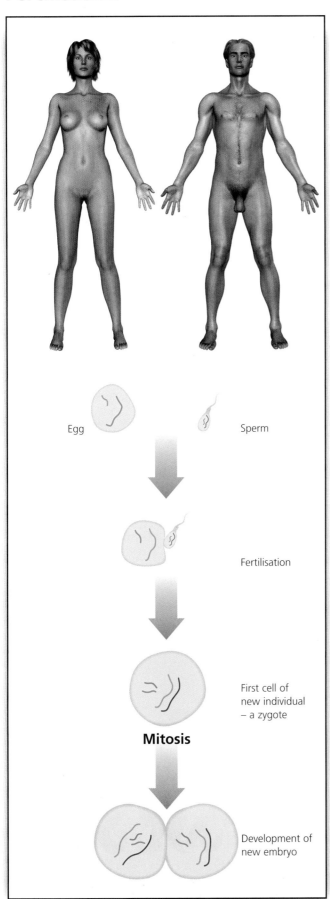

Egg

Sperm

Fertilisation

First cell of new individual – a zygote

Mitosis

Development of new embryo

During fertilisation, a male gamete (sperm) and a female gamete (egg) fuse together.

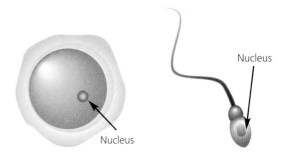

Nucleus

Nucleus

It is important that the cells produced during meiosis only have half the number of chromosomes as the parent cell, so when they fuse they produce a single body cell, called a **zygote**, with one whole set of chromosomes. In each pair of chromosomes, one chromosome comes from the father and one chromosome comes from the mother.

The zygote divides by mitosis to produce a cluster of cells called an embryo. The cells of the embryo all contain the same DNA. These cells will eventually differentiate into bone, muscle and nerve cells, etc.

The cells of the embryo also have to ensure that different tissues develop at the correct stages.

The embryo continues to develop by mitosis (from 1 cell to 2, to 4, to 8, etc.) to eventually become an adult individual. An adult human contains approximately 1×10^{14} (100 trillion) cells.

Each cell has the same information copied inside the nucleus.

Variation

Meiosis and sexual reproduction produce variation between offspring and parents because, when the gametes fuse, genetic information from two individuals is combined.

For each gene, just one of each parent's two alleles is passed on. This means that each offspring can have a different combination of alleles from either parent and, therefore, different characteristics.

This process is completely random.

Growth and Development

Controlling Growth and Development

Growth and development in organisms are governed by genes present on the chromosomes in each cell nucleus. Genes determine characteristics (e.g. the ability to roll your tongue) by providing instructions for the production of proteins, and therefore control the development of the whole organism.

The instructions are in the form of a code, made up of four bases which hold the two strands of the molecule together. These bases always pair up in the same way (i.e. form the same base pairs):

- adenine (A) pairs with thymine (T)
- cytosine (C) pairs with guanine (G).

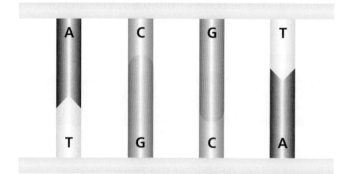

The chromosomes (and the genes that are on them) always stay inside the nucleus. However, the production of proteins takes place outside the nucleus, in the cytoplasm.

Therefore, there is a mechanism for transferring the information stored in the genes into the cytoplasm.

Imagine the nucleus is a reference library, from which you are not allowed to remove the books. You would need to copy down any information you needed so that you could take it away with you.

The DNA cannot leave the cell because it is too large. So, the relevant section of DNA is unzipped and the instructions are copied onto smaller molecules called **messenger RNA** (mRNA). These leave the nucleus and carry the instructions to the **ribosomes** which follow the instructions to make the relevant protein.

HT The sequence of bases in a gene determines the order in which amino acids are joined together to make a particular protein. A group of three base pairs codes for one amino acid in a protein chain (this is called a triplet code). There are 20 different amino acids that can be used.

The process culminates in a protein, its structure is dependent upon the amino acids that make it up.

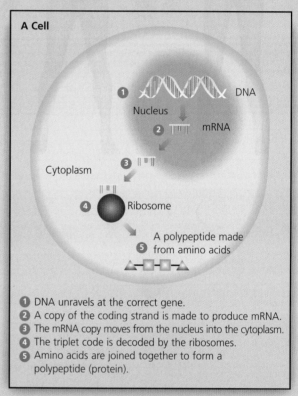

1. DNA unravels at the correct gene.
2. A copy of the coding strand is made to produce mRNA.
3. The mRNA copy moves from the nucleus into the cytoplasm.
4. The triplet code is decoded by the ribosomes.
5. Amino acids are joined together to form a polypeptide (protein).

The diagram below shows an example of a protein. The different coloured shapes represent different amino acid chains which give the protein its characteristic shape.

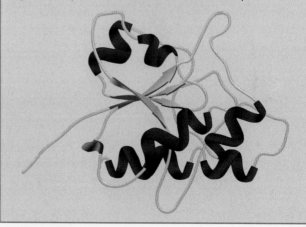

Growth and Development

Development of New Organisms

In a human embryo, all the cells are identical up to the 8 cell stage and could potentially develop into any sort of cell required by the organism, including neurons, blood cells, liver cells or muscle cells. These identical cells are known as **embryonic stem cells**.

At the 16 cell stage (approximately 4 days after fertilisation) the cells in an embryo begin to specialise and form different types of tissue. The cells contain the same genetic information, but each cell's position relative to the others is different. The distribution of various proteins in the egg cell is also different, so although embryonic cells contain the same genes, the cells are already different from one another. At the time of specialisation, these differences determine what specific function a cell will have.

The only genes that are active in a cell are the ones that are needed by that cell. The cell only produces the specific proteins it needs to enable it to carry out its role. Some proteins are needed by all cells, whilst others will only be needed in specific cells.

In human DNA, there are approximately 20 000 to 25 000 genes. This means that a similar number of proteins can be manufactured in the human body.

Stem Cells

Stem cells could potentially be used to help treat diseases and disorders, and to repair damage to various tissues. Although there are lots of benefits associated with stem cell technology, there are also a number of **ethical issues** (see p.10).

There are three sources of stem cells – embryos, blood from the umbilical cord and **adult stem cells**. Only the embryonic stem cells are completely unspecialised and can be used to form any cell type.

Therapeutic cloning is a process which involves removing the nucleus from an egg cell and replacing it with a nucleus from one of the patient's cells. The egg cell is then stimulated so that it starts to divide (as if it were a zygote).

At the 8 cell stage, cells can be removed as they are still unspecialised. However, this technique is highly controversial because, effectively, a clone of the adult patient is being created, although it is prevented from developing to adult form.

Adult stem cells are not like embryonic stem cells – they will only produce cells of a certain type (rather than any cell), e.g. cells for creating blood cells in bone marrow would have to be encouraged to grow more of that type of cell by reactivating inactive genes in the nuclei.

The problem here is that there is only a small proportion of these cells amongst lots of non-stem cells so they are difficult to harvest. The reactivation process itself is also difficult.

To date, scientists have successfully grown ears, skin and, most recently, a bladder, using the patients' own cells. They can either be grown in a laboratory, or by using a 'host animal' to maintain a blood supply during growth.

The advantage of using adult cells is that they can be taken from the patient, so the patient's immune system will not reject the transplant.

Human ear grown on the back of a mouse. The mouse provides all the blood vessels needed to keep the ear alive.

Growth and Development

Differentiation in Plants

Plant cells, as with animal cells, divide by the process of mitosis. The cells then specialise into the cells of roots, leaves or flowers. Unlike animals, most plants continue to grow in height and width throughout their lives.

Meristems

Plant growth occurs in areas called **meristems**, which are sites where unspecialised cells divide repeatedly (mitosis). These cells then differentiate, and become specialised in relation to the function they will perform.

There are two types of meristems: those that result in increased girth (**lateral**) and those that result in increased height and longer roots (**apical**).

Cells from the meristem behave like embryonic stem cells in animals – they can develop into any type of plant cell. The presence of these unspecialised cells is what enables clones of plants with desirable features to be produced from cuttings.

Clones can be produced by growing cells from the meristem in a special culture medium (jelly containing relevant nutrients) to produce a **callus**, which is a cluster of undifferentiated cells containing the same genetic information as the parent plant.

If the hormonal conditions in their environment are changed, these unspecialised plant cells can develop into a range of other tissues such as xylem and phloem (see p.49), or organs such as leaves, roots and flowers.

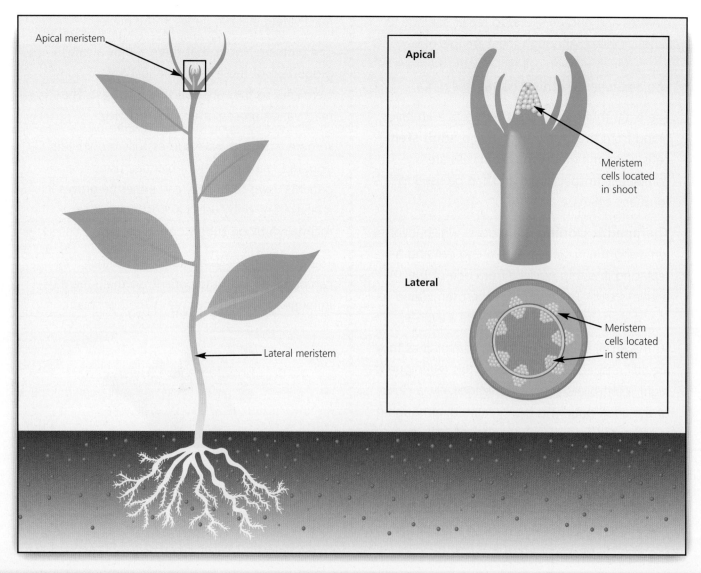

Apical meristem

Lateral meristem

Apical

Meristem cells located in shoot

Lateral

Meristem cells located in stem

Growth and Development

Xylem and Phloem

Xylem are used by the plant to transport water and soluble mineral salts from the roots to the stem and leaves, and to replace water lost during transpiration and photosynthesis. By adding certain plant hormones to unspecialised plant cells, xylem tissue can be formed.

Phloem, the tubes used by the plant to transport dissolved food to the whole plant for respiration or storage, can be generated in a similar way to xylem (see diagram opposite).

Cuttings

Plants can be reproduced by taking a cutting and putting it in a rooting hormone which causes roots to form. Because the cutting already has a stem and leaves it will develop into a complete new plant, which is genetically identical to the parent plant (i.e. it is a clone).

> **HT** There are a wide range of plant hormones. The main group that is used in horticulture is called **auxins**. Auxins mainly affect cell division at the tip of a shoot, because this is where cell division mainly occurs. Just under the tip, the cells grow in size under the influence of auxins, causing the stem or root to grow longer.

Responding to Stimuli

All living organisms possess sensitivity. For example, plants are able to respond to changes in their environment. They can respond to external stimuli such as gravity or light by changing the direction of growth.

The mechanism by which plants respond to light is called **phototropism**. A plant's survival depends on its ability to photosynthesise; it needs light to grow. Plants, therefore, need strategies to detect light and respond to changes in intensity. This is demonstrated by the way in which plants will grow towards a light source (see diagram opposite).

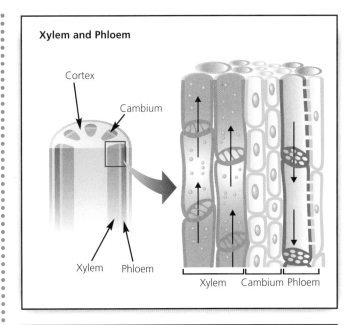

Xylem and Phloem

Cortex
Cambium
Xylem Phloem
Xylem Cambium Phloem

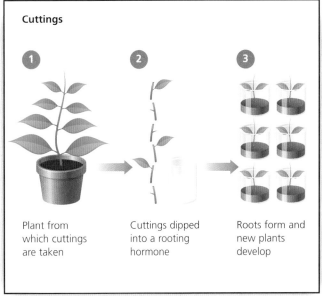

Cuttings

1. Plant from which cuttings are taken
2. Cuttings dipped into a rooting hormone
3. Roots form and new plants develop

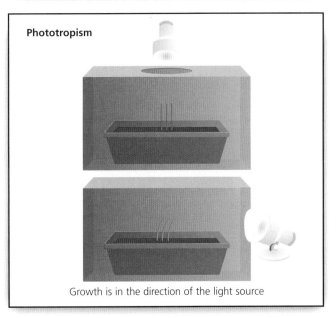

Phototropism

Growth is in the direction of the light source

Growth and Development

How Phototropism Works

The cells which are furthest away from a light source grow more, due to the presence of auxin, which is sensitive to light.

Auxin is produced at the shoot tip and migrates down the shoot.

If a light source is directly overhead, then the distribution of auxin would be the same on both sides of the plant shoot.

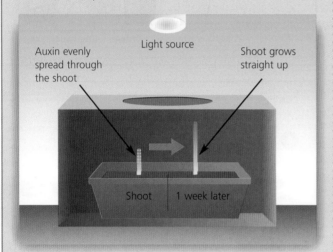

If a light source shines onto the shoot at an angle, the auxin at the tip moves away from the light source.

As a result, the concentration of auxin on the side furthest away from the light increases, causing the cells there to elongate, and the shoot begins to bend towards the light.

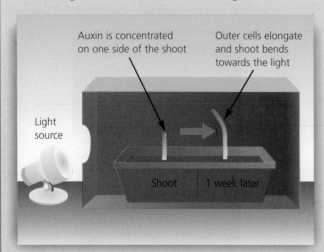

Charles Darwin carried out some simple experiments that demonstrated the role played by plant hormones produced in the shoot tip.

As we have seen, light causes the shoot to bend towards the source. If the tip of the shoot is removed or covered in opaque material then the plant will continue to grow upwards – as if the light source was not there.

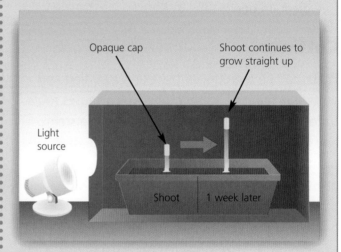

If the tip is covered with a transparent cap then it will still grow towards the light source. The same thing will happen if an opaque cylinder is wrapped around the stem leaving the tip exposed.

This experiment proves it is a substance produced in the tip that caused the cells further down the shoot to grow.

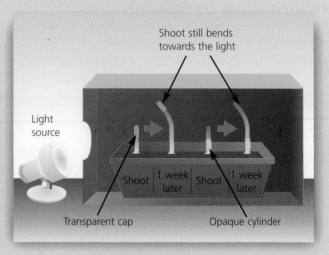

Module B6

How the human brain functions remains largely unknown. Neuroscience (the study of the nervous system, including the brain) is an area at the forefront of medical research, as developments and discoveries in this field have a huge potential impact for society. This module looks at…

- how organisms respond to changes in their environment
- how information is passed through the nervous system
- what reflex actions are
- how humans develop more complex behaviour
- what we know about the way in which the brain coordinates our senses
- how drugs affect our nervous system
- stem cells, and their role in treating disease.

Changes in Environment

Most living organisms can detect and respond to **stimuli**, i.e. changes, in their environment.

Animals respond to stimuli in order to keep themselves in conditions that will ensure their survival. These responses are coordinated by the **central nervous system (CNS)**.

The pathway for receiving information and then acting upon it is…

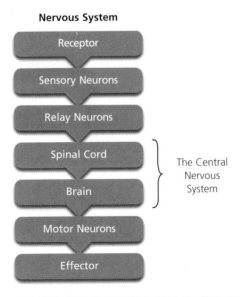

Nervous System

Receptor → Sensory Neurons → Relay Neurons → Spinal Cord → Brain → Motor Neurons → Effector

(Spinal Cord and Brain: The Central Nervous System)

The Central Nervous System

The central nervous system allows organisms to react to their surroundings and coordinates their responses.

Remember, the central nervous system (brain and spinal cord) is connected to the body via sensory and motor neurons, which make the **peripheral nervous system** (**PNS**).

The peripheral nervous system is the second major division of the nervous system.

Its sensory and motor neurons transmit messages all over the body, for example, to the limbs and organs.

They also transmit messages to and from the central nervous system.

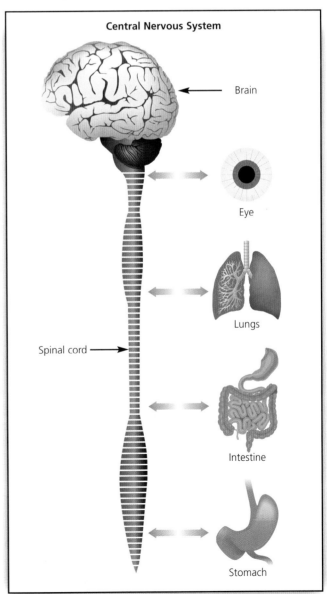

Central Nervous System

Brain

Eye

Lungs

Spinal cord

Intestine

Stomach

Brain and Mind

Sensory neurons carry nervous impulses (electrical signals) from receptors to the CNS.

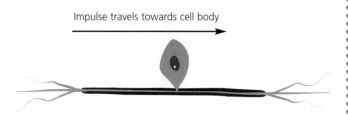

Impulse travels towards cell body

Motor neurons carry impulses from the CNS to effectors.

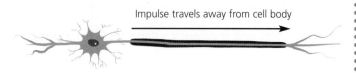

Impulse travels away from cell body

Types of Receptor

- **Light** – receptors in the eyes.
- **Sound** – receptors in the ears.
- **Change of position** – receptors in the ears (balance).
- **Taste** – receptors on the tongue.
- **Smell** – receptors in the nose.
- **Touch, pressure and temperature** – receptors in the skin.

Receptors and Effectors

Receptors and effectors can form part of complex organs:

1 Muscle cells in muscle tissue

The specialised cells that make up muscle tissues are effectors. Impulses travel along motor neurons and terminate at the muscle cells. These impulses cause the muscle cells to contract.

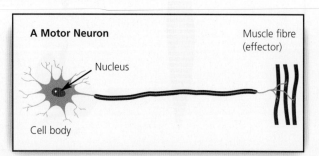

A Motor Neuron

Muscle fibre (effector)

Nucleus

Cell body

2 Light receptors in the retina of the eye

The eye is a complex sense organ. The lens focuses light onto receptor cells in the retina which are sensitive to light. The receptor cells are then stimulated and send impulses along sensory neurons to the brain.

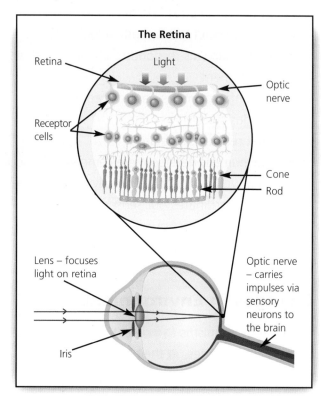

The Retina

Retina

Light

Optic nerve

Receptor cells

Cone

Rod

Lens – focuses light on retina

Optic nerve – carries impulses via sensory neurons to the brain

Iris

3 Hormone-secreting cells in a gland

The hormone-secreting cells in glands are effectors. They are activated by an impulse, which travels along a motor neuron from the CNS and terminates at the gland. The impulse triggers the release of the hormone into the bloodstream, which transports it to the site where it is required.

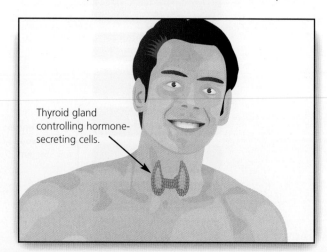

Thyroid gland controlling hormone-secreting cells.

Neurons

Neurons are specially adapted cells that can carry an **electrical signal** when stimulated, e.g. a **nerve impulse**. They are **elongated** (lengthened) to make connections from one part of the body to another. They have **branched endings** which allow a single neuron to act on many other neurons or effectors, e.g. muscle fibres.

In **motor neurons** the cytoplasm forms a long fibre surrounded by a cell membrane called an **axon**.

Some axons are surrounded by a fatty sheath, which insulates the neuron from neighbouring cells (a bit like the plastic coating on an electrical wire) and increases the speed at which the nerve impulse is transmitted.

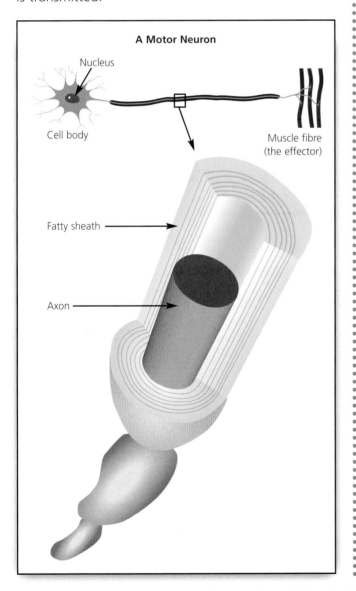

A Motor Neuron

Nucleus

Cell body

Muscle fibre (the effector)

Fatty sheath

Axon

Synapses

Synapses are the gaps between adjacent neurons. They allow the brain to form interconnected neural circuits. The human brain contains a huge number of synapses. There are approximately 1000 trillion in a young child. This number decreases with age, stabilising by adulthood. The estimated number of synapses for an adult human varies between 100 and 500 trillion.

HT When an impulse reaches the end of a sensory neuron, it triggers the release of chemicals, called neurotransmitters, into the synapse. They diffuse across the synapse and bind with receptor molecules on the membrane of a motor neuron.

The receptor molecules bind with certain chemicals to initiate a nerve impulse in the motor neuron so the signal can continue on its way. Meanwhile, the neurotransmitter is reabsorbed back into the sensory neuron, to be used again.

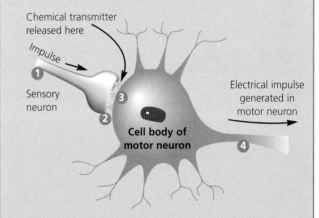

Chemical transmitter released here

Impulse

Sensory neuron

Cell body of motor neuron

Electrical impulse generated in motor neuron

The sequence is as follows.
1. Electrical signal (nerve impulse) moves through sensory neuron.
2. Chemicals (neurotransmitters) are released into synapse.
3. Neurotransmitters bind with receptors on motor neuron.
4. Electrical signal (nerve impulse) is sent through motor neuron.

Brain and Mind

Reflex Actions

When certain receptors are stimulated they cause a very fast, involuntarily (automatic) response.

These simple reflexes involve both sensory and motor neurons. The basic pathway for a simple reflex arc is shown below:

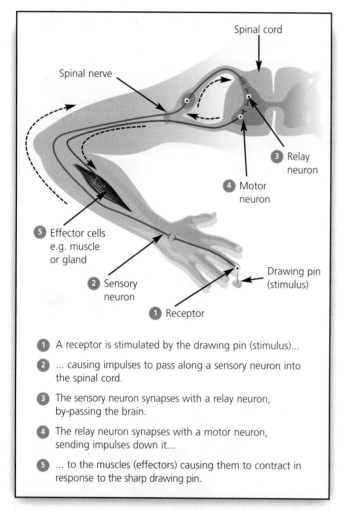

1. A receptor is stimulated by the drawing pin (stimulus)...

2. ... causing impulses to pass along a sensory neuron into the spinal cord.

3. The sensory neuron synapses with a relay neuron, by-passing the brain.

4. The relay neuron synapses with a motor neuron, sending impulses down it...

5. ... to the muscles (effectors) causing them to contract in response to the sharp drawing pin.

In animals, simple reflexes like these are an important part of self-preservation; the animal will automatically respond to a stimulus in a way that helps it to survive, for example, by finding food, sheltering from predators, finding a mate or avoiding injury.

A majority of the behaviour displayed by simple animals, e.g. insects, is the result of reflex actions. For example, a woodlouse responds to changes in light brand humidity by automatically moving towards damp, dark places. The disadvantage of this type of behaviour is that the animals have difficulty responding to new situations.

Simple Reflexes in Humans

Newborn babies exhibit a range of simple reflexes for a short time after birth. The absence of these reflexes, or their failure to disappear, might indicate that the nervous system is not developing properly.

- **Stepping reflex** – when held under its arms in an upright position with feet on a firm surface, a baby makes walking movements with legs.
- **Startle (or moro) reflex** – baby shoots out arms and legs when startled, e.g. by a loud noise.
- **Grasping reflex** – baby tightly grasps a finger that is placed in its hand.
- **Rooting reflex** – baby turns head and opens mouth ready to feed when its cheek is stroked.
- **Sucking reflex** – baby sucks on a finger (or mother's nipple) that is put in its mouth.

Adults also display a range of simple reflexes. For example, the pupil reflex in the eye stops bright light from damaging the very sensitive cells that line the retina.

The iris of an eye consists of muscle tissue and, by contracting various muscle fibres, it can control the size of the pupil and, therefore, the amount of light entering the eye.

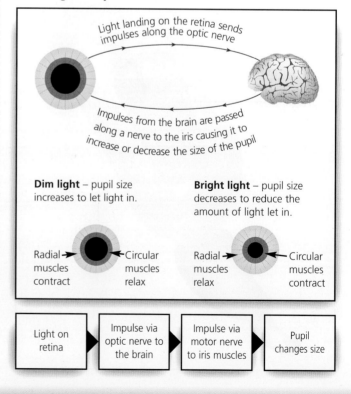

Conditioned Reflexes

Although they are not conscious actions, reflex responses to a new stimulus can be learnt. Through a process called conditioning, the body learns to produce a specific reflex response when a certain stimulus is detected. Conditioning works by building an association between the new stimulus (the **secondary stimulus**) and the stimulus that naturally triggers the response (the **primary stimulus**). This resulting reflex is called a **conditioned reflex action**.

This effect was discovered at the beginning of the 20th century by a Russian Scientist named Pavlov, who received the Nobel prize for his work.

Pavlov observed that whenever a dog sees and smells a piece of meat, it starts to salivate (produce saliva). In his experiment, a bell was rung repeatedly whenever meat was shown and given to the dog. Eventually, simply ringing the bell, without any meat present, caused the dog to salivate. This classic experiment is known as Pavlov's dog experiment.

Simple Reflex

Meat ➡ Salivation

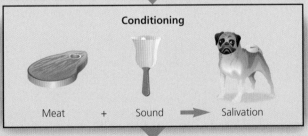

Conditioning

Meat + Sound ➡ Salivation

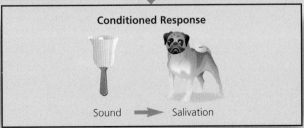

Conditioned Response

Sound ➡ Salivation

In a conditioned reflex the final response has no direct connection to the stimulus.

For example, the ringing bell in Pavlov's experiment is a stimulus that has *nothing* to do with feeding; it is just a sound. However, the association between the sound of the bell and meat is strong enough to induce the dog to salivate.

Some conditioned reflexes can increase a species' chance of survival:

Example

The caterpillar of the cinnabar moth is black and orange in colour, to warn predators that it is poisonous. After eating a few cinnabar caterpillars, a bird will start to associate these colours with a very unpleasant taste and avoid eating anything that is black and orange in colour.

In some situations the brain can override or modify a reflex action.

For example, when the hand comes into contact with something that is hot, the body's natural reflex response is to pull away or drop the object.

However, you might know an object is hot but still want to pick it up, e.g. a hot potato or a dinner plate. To allow you to do this, the brain sends a signal, via a neuron, to the motor neuron in the reflex arc, modifying the reflex so that you do not drop the potato or plate.

Brain and Mind

Complex Behaviour

Mammals have a **complex brain** which contains billions of neurons (nerve cells). This allows them to learn from experience, including how to respond to different situations (social behaviour).

Rabbits learn quite quickly that eating stinging nettles is painful; dogs can be trained to respond to instructions or to hunt for explosives; horses or cattle that are reared alone will often be vicious fighters when mixed with other animals – they adapt to being alone rather than part of a herd. All these aspects of behaviour are due to the ability of the brain to adapt and respond.

In mammals, **neuron pathways** are formed in the brain during development. The way in which the animal interacts with its environment determines what pathways are formed.

During the first few years after birth, the brain grows extremely rapidly. As each neuron matures, it sends out multiple branches, increasing the number of synapses (junctions between neurons).

At birth, in humans, the cerebral cortex (see p.57) has approximately 2 500 synapses per neuron. By the time an infant is two or three years old, the number of synapses is approximately 15 000 synapses per neuron.

Each time an individual has a new experience, a different pathway between neurons is stimulated. Every time the experience is repeated after that, the pathway is strengthened. Pathways which are not used regularly are eventually deleted. Only the pathways that are activated most frequently are preserved.

These modifications mean that certain pathways of the brain become more likely to transmit impulses than others and the individual will become better at a given task. This is why some skills may be learnt through repetition. For example, riding a bicycle, revising for an exam, learning to ski or playing a musical instrument.

The average adult brain has approximately half the amount of synapses of an infant brain.

The brain's ability to reorganise neural pathways in this way throughout its lifetime is called **plasticity**.

A PET scan (an imaging technique which produces 3-D images) shows neuron activity in parts of the brain in response to learning words through speaking, hearing and seeing them. The areas which are stimulated the most will develop a greater number of synapses between neurons.

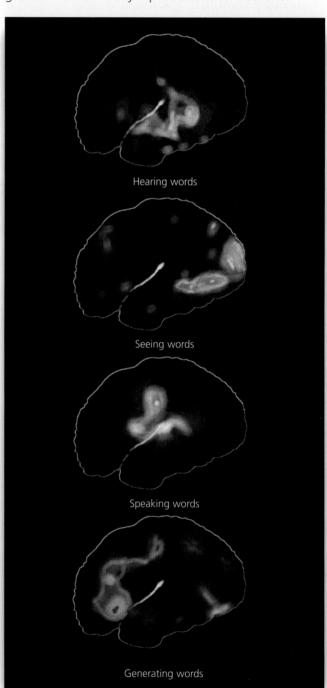

Hearing words

Seeing words

Speaking words

Generating words

HT Feral Children

If neural pathways are not used then they are destroyed. There is evidence to suggest that because of this, if a new skill, e.g. language, has not been learnt by a particular stage in development, an animal or child might not be able to learn it in the same way as normal.

One example of evidence showing this comes from the study of so-called 'feral children' (feral means wild).

Feral children are children who have been isolated from society in some way, so they do not go through the normal development process. This can be deliberate (e.g. inhumanely keeping a child in isolation in a cellar or locked room) or it can be accidental (e.g. through being shipwrecked).

In the absence of any other humans, the children do not ever gain the ability to talk (or may lose any ability already gained) other than to make rudimentary grunting noises. Learning a language later in development is a much harder and slower process.

Child Development

After children are born there are a series of developmental milestones which can be checked to see if development is following normal patterns.

If they are missing or late it could mean that there are neurological problems, or it could mean that the child is lacking stimulation (is not being exposed to the necessary experiences). For example, at three months, babies should be able to lift their heads when held to someone's shoulder, or grasp a rattle when it is given to them.

By 12 months, babies should be able to hold a cup and drink from it, and walk when one of their hands is held.

Adapting

The variety of potential pathways in the brain makes it possible for animals to adapt to new situations. For example, dogs can be trained to follow spoken commands and even sniff out drugs and explosives.

Marine animals in captivity such as dolphins and killer whales can be trained to collect food from a person's hand or to push underwater buttons that will release food.

Coordination of Senses

The cerebral cortex is the part of the human brain that is most concerned with intelligence, memory, language and consciousness.

Cerebral cortex

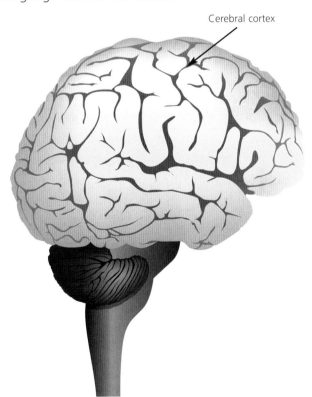

Brain and Mind

Mapping the Cortex

Scientists have used a variety of methods to map the different regions of the cerebral cortex:

- **Physiological Techniques**

  Damage to different parts of the brain can produce different problems, e.g. long-term memory loss, short-term memory loss, paralysis in one or more parts of the body, speech loss, etc. Therefore, studying the effects of accidents or illnesses on the brain has led to an understanding of which parts of the brain control different functions:

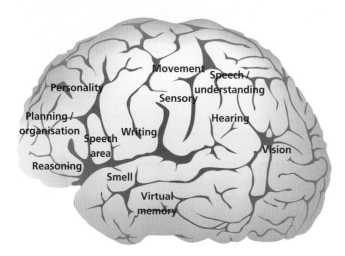

N.B. You do not need to learn the different parts of the brain.

- **Electronic Techniques**

  An **electroencephalogram** (EEG) is a visual record of the electrical activity generated by neurons in the brain. By placing electrodes on the scalp and amplifying the electrical signals picked up through the skull, a trace can be produced showing the rise and fall of electrical potentials called brain waves.

  By stimulating the patient's receptors (e.g. by flashing lights or making sounds), the parts of the brain which respond can be mapped.

  Magnetic Resonance Imaging (MRI) scanning is a relatively new technique that can be used to produce images of different cross-sections of the brain. The computer-generated picture uses colour to represent different levels of electrical activity. The activity in the brain changes depending on what the person is doing or thinking.

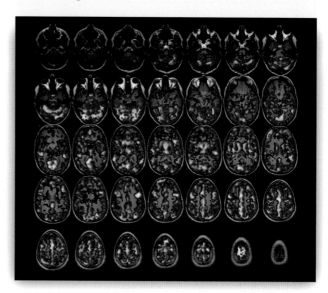

Memory

Memory is the ability to store and retrieve information. Scientists have produced models to try to explain how the brain facilitates this but, so far, none have been able to provide an adequate explanation.

Verbal memory (words and labels) can be divided into **short-term memory** and **long-term memory**. Short-term memory is capable of storing a limited amount of information for a limited amount of time (roughly 15–30 seconds). Long-term memory can store a seemingly unlimited amount of information indefinitely.

When using short-term memory, it is believed that up to 7 (+/-2) separate pieces of information can be stored (e.g. a number with seven digits like 6421978). This capacity can be increased by dividing information into small chunks, e.g. (213) (645) (978) could be stored as 3 out of the possible 7 units of storage.

Long-term memory is where information is stored in the brain through repetition, which strengthens and builds up the neuron pathway.

More on Memory

Humans are more likely to remember information when…

- it is repeated (especially over an extended period of time), e.g. going over key points several times as a method of revising for exams
- there is a strong stimulus associated with it, including colour, light, smell or sound (the more senses involved the better)
- there is a pattern to it (or if a pattern can be artificially imposed on it). For example, people find remembering the order of the planets difficult, so a sentence where there is a logical relationship between the words (unlike the names of the planets themselves) can be remembered as a prompt instead: **m**y **v**ery **e**asy **m**ethod **j**ust **s**peeds **u**p **n**aming **p**lanets – **M**ercury, **V**enus, **E**arth, **M**ars, **J**upiter, **S**aturn, **U**ranus, **N**eptune and **P**luto. This is called a mnemonic and is an example of an artificially imposed pattern.

Drugs and the Nervous System

Many drugs cause changes in the speed at which nerve impulses travel to the brain, speeding them up or slowing them down. False signals are sometimes sent.

Drugs and toxins (poisons) can prevent impulses from travelling across synapses, or they can cause the nervous system to become overloaded with too many impulses.

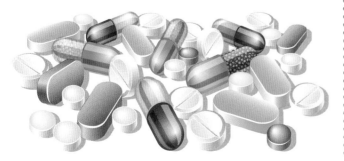

For example, alcohol has a direct effect on chemical transmitters in the brain. The more alcohol that is consumed, the slower the chemical signals are sent, and so coordination and reaction times decrease.

Caffeine, in low doses, causes nerve impulses to be sent faster and therefore increases reaction times.

Serotonin is a chemical transmitter (neurotransmitter) used in the central nervous system. It can have mood-enhancing effects, i.e. it is associated with feeling happy.

Serotonin passes across the brain's synapses, landing on receptor molecules.

Serotonin not on a receptor is absorbed back into the transmitting neuron by the transporter molecules. Ecstasy (MDMA) blocks the sites in the brain's synapses where the chemical serotonin is removed.

As a result, serotonin concentrations in the brain increase and the user experiences feelings of elation. However, the neurons are harmed in this process and a long-term consequence of taking Ecstasy can be memory loss.

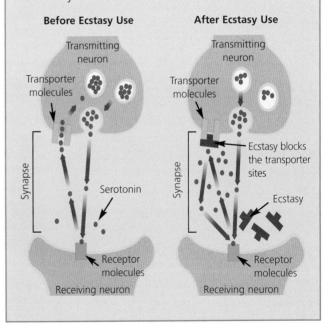

Further Biology

Further biology provides an opportunity to study selected topics in depth. This module looks at…

- food chains and pyramids
- soil and biomass
- relationships between organisms
- genetic modification
- blood groups
- injuries and treatments.

Energy and Organisms

All living things on Earth ultimately get their energy from the Sun's radiation. A small proportion of this energy is absorbed by green plants during **photosynthesis**.

The Sun's energy is stored in chemicals (e.g. starch, lignin, chlorophyll, etc.) that make up plants' cells. When the plants, and the animals that eat them, are eaten or decompose, the energy is then transferred to other organisms. Decay organisms can feed off dead organisms and the waste products of animals.

Autotrophs and Heterotrophs

Autotrophs (self feeders) are organisms that make their own food. Plants (also known as producers) are autotrophs.

Heterotrophs are organisms that are unable to make their own food so instead they obtain their energy by **consuming** other organisms. Animals and decay organisms (including some bacteria and fungi) are heterotrophs.

Animals that eat plants are called **herbivores** and are **primary consumers**. Animals that eat other animals are called **carnivores** and may be **secondary** or even **tertiary consumers**.

An **ecosystem** is a defined area containing a self-sustained community of organisms (autotrophs and heterotrophs) living in the non-living surroundings, e.g. a pond or a wood. The transfer of food energy in an ecosystem can be represented in a number of ways, including…

- food chains
- pyramids of numbers
- pyramids of biomass.

Food Chains

Energy in a food chain always flows in one direction.

1 It starts with light energy from the **Sun**.

2 The light energy then transfers to an **autotroph**, which captures the energy, carries out photosynthesis and stores the energy in its cells.

3 A **herbivore heterotroph** then eats the autotroph. Some of the energy stored in the plant is transferred to the herbivore and stored in its cells.

4 A **carnivore heterotroph** then eats the herbivore heterotroph. Some of the energy is transferred to the carnivore and stored in its cells.

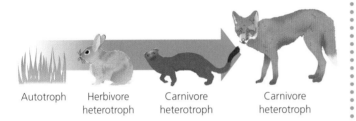

| Autotroph | Herbivore heterotroph | Carnivore heterotroph | Carnivore heterotroph |

At each stage of the food chain, a large proportion of the energy is…

- lost to the environment as heat or through respiration
- excreted as waste products
- trapped in undigestable material such as bones and fur.

This means that as the food chain moves from autotrophs to heterotrophs, there is **less energy** available at each **trophic level** (i.e. each stage in the food chain). Therefore, there is a **limit** to the number of levels in each food chain – usually around four or five levels.

Pyramids of Numbers

A **pyramid of numbers** can be used to show the total number of organisms that feed on each other in a food chain. Each horizontal level of the pyramid represents a trophic level. By looking at these levels we can understand the feeding relationships and numbers of autotrophs and heterotrophs.

The chart is called a pyramid because typically the bottom bar (showing the number of autotrophs consumed) will be the largest, and the top bar (showing the top consumer) will be the smallest. This is because only some of the energy and nutrients are passed on from consumer to consumer.

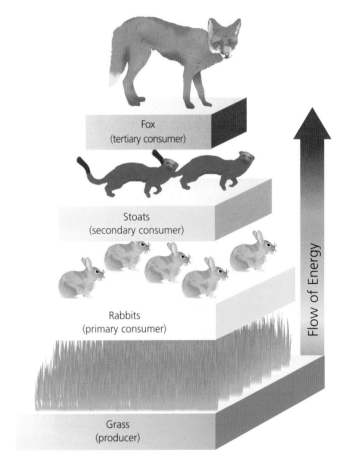

Fox (tertiary consumer)

Stoats (secondary consumer)

Rabbits (primary consumer)

Grass (producer)

Flow of Energy

However, pyramids of numbers can have unusual shapes. For example, one oak tree might have many aphids feeding on it, so the bar representing the oak tree will be smaller than the one representing the aphids.

If the aphids are then eaten by blue tits, and kestrels eat the blue tits, the resulting pyramid would look like this:

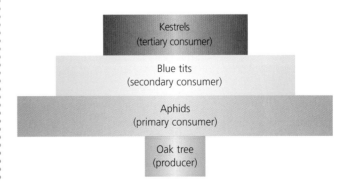

Kestrels (tertiary consumer)

Blue tits (secondary consumer)

Aphids (primary consumer)

Oak tree (producer)

Further Biology

Pyramids of Biomass

A more effective (and accurate) way of representing the feeding relationships is to draw a **pyramid of biomass**.

Each horizontal bar still represents an organism at each stage of the food chain, but instead of recording the **numbers** of individuals at each level, the pyramid of biomass relies on the **biomass**. (The biomass is the total mass of organisms at each trophic level at a particular time.)

The biomass at each stage of a food chain will be less than it was at the previous stage.

The advantage of pyramids of biomass is that, by drawing the biomass at each stage to scale, the pyramid will always retain a pyramidal shape, reducing the chance of making mistakes in interpretation.

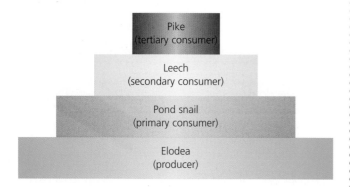

Calculating Energy Efficiency

You need to be able to calculate the energy efficiency at each stage of the food chain. This could mean using data from…

- a food chain
- a pyramid of numbers or a pyramid of biomass
- an arrow diagram showing energy changes.

The percentage of energy efficiency can be calculated using the following formula:

$$\text{Percentage of energy transferred} = \frac{\text{Input energy}}{\text{Output energy}} \times 100$$

Example

The arrow diagram below shows the feeding relationship between a green plant, a caterpillar and a bird.

Calculate how efficient the energy transfer is for the caterpillar feeding on the plant.

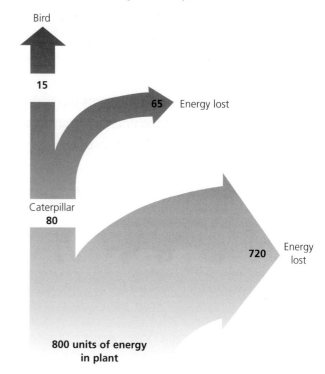

$$\text{Percentage of energy transferred} = \frac{\text{Input energy}}{\text{Output energy}} \times 100$$

$$= \frac{80}{800} \times 100$$

$$= \textbf{10\%}$$

N.B. On average only 10% of energy from the Sun ends up stored as plant tissue. If an animal eats a plant, 10% of the energy gained is used to build up muscle. The rest of the energy is used by the animal to respire, move and keep warm.

Soil

Soil is the upper, weathered layer of the Earth's surface, no more than 2m deep. Soil is comprised of several things:

- **Biomass**, which is made up of…
  - living organisms (e.g. microorganisms such as bacteria, Nematode worms and fungi, and larger organisms such as mites and earthworms)
  - decaying organic material (e.g. leaf litter, dead animals, etc.).
- **Inorganic material**, i.e. bits of rock, stones and minerals, which give structure to the soil, allow air to get in and out, and retain water.
- **Air** (oxygen in air pockets), which organisms use for aerobic respiration. Over-compressing or water-logging the soil can remove the air pockets, which reduces the variety of organisms that can survive in the soil.
- **Water**, which in small quantities helps animals and plants to grow. There may be **dissolved mineral** ions in the water, such as nitrates and phosphates which are useful for plants and other organisms. Plant roots absorb the mineral ions, as well as adding support and structure to the soil.

Nitrate Absorption

Plants need to absorb nitrates from the soil for healthy growth. Plants normally absorb nutrients by diffusion, but the concentration of nitrates outside the plant is lower than that inside. Therefore, a plant has to **use energy** to absorb nitrates by **active transport** (see p. 37).

Calculating Water Mass and Biomass

The **percentage mass of water** in a soil sample can be calculated by first measuring the mass of the fresh soil (wet mass). The soil is then heated until the water has evaporated and the mass is measured again (dry mass).

The following calculations are then carried out:

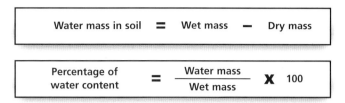

$$\text{Water mass in soil} = \text{Wet mass} - \text{Dry mass}$$

$$\text{Percentage of water content} = \frac{\text{Water mass}}{\text{Wet mass}} \times 100$$

Similar procedures are used to find the **biomass content** of soil samples. To find the oven dry mass, the sample is heated in an oven for a long time to burn off the organic material.

Biomass can be found using the following calculations:

$$\text{Biomass} = \text{Wet mass} - \text{Oven dry mass}$$

$$\text{Percentage of biomass} = \frac{\text{Biomass}}{\text{Wet mass}} \times 100$$

Example – Calculating Water Mass

Niamh collected soil samples to analyse. She measured Soil A and found that it had a wet mass of 98g. She dried the sample in an oven and then measured the dry mass as 57g. Calculate the percentage water content of the soil.

Water mass = Wet mass – Dry mass

$$= 98g - 57g = \mathbf{41g}$$

$$\text{Percentage of water content} = \frac{\text{Water mass}}{\text{Wet mass}} \times 100$$

$$= \frac{41}{98} \times 100 = \mathbf{42\%}$$

Example – Calculating Biomass

Niamh then wanted to calculate the amount of biomass in her soil sample. The mass of the sample after heating in an oven was 39g. Calculate the biomass.

Biomass = Wet mass – Oven dry mass

$$= 98g - 39g = \mathbf{59g}$$

$$\text{Percentage of biomass} = \frac{\text{Biomass}}{\text{Wet mass}} \times 100$$

$$= \frac{59g}{98g} \times 100 = \mathbf{60\%}$$

Further Biology

Photosynthesis

The process of photosynthesis can be summarised by this equation:

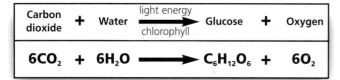

Carbon dioxide	+	Water	$\xrightarrow[\text{chlorophyll}]{\text{light energy}}$	Glucose	+	Oxygen
$6CO_2$	+	$6H_2O$	$\longrightarrow$	$C_6H_{12}O_6$	+	$6O_2$

Photosynthesis takes place in three stages:

1. Light energy (from the Sun) is absorbed by a chemical called **chlorophyll** in green plants. (Chlorophyll is not used up in the process, and it is not a reactant.)
2. Within the chlorophyll molecule, the light energy is used to rearrange the atoms of carbon dioxide and water to produce glucose (a sugar).
3. Oxygen is produced as a waste product. It exits the plant via the leaf or can be reused by the plant during respiration.

Energy Use in Plants

Glucose can be used in respiration to release energy for the plant in order for other chemical reactions to take place.

Glucose can be converted into chemicals that are needed for plant cell growth, for example…

- carbohydrates (such as cellulose and starch)
- protein
- chlorophyll.

Glucose is a soluble chemical that can be stored in a plant as an insoluble long-chained carbohydrate molecule called **starch**. Long-chained molecules that are made up of many copies of the same unit are called **polymers**.

Starch is a polymer as it is made up of millions of glucose molecules joined together.

Glucose	Starch
Individual sugar molecules	Long chains of identical sugar molecules

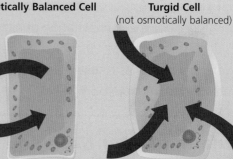

Cellulose is another example of a carbohydrate. It is needed by the plant to build cell walls. It has a similar structure to starch but the long chains are cross-linked to form a mesh.

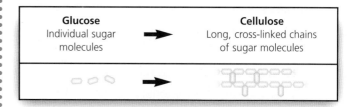

Glucose	Cellulose
Individual sugar molecules	Long, cross-linked chains of sugar molecules

Glucose, together with nitrates absorbed by the soil, can be converted into **amino acids**. Amino acids can be linked together in different combinations to make **proteins**, another example of a polymer.

Ⓗ Storing Starch

Cells contain water. If glucose dissolves in the cell water, it changes the **osmotic balance** of the cell to favour net water movement into the cell.

If a plant cell does not contain any dissolved glucose, water moves in and out at the same rate, so it is osmotically balanced.

If a plant cell contains dissolved glucose, the less-concentrated water outside the cell will flow into the cell by osmosis. This causes the cell to swell (become turgid). The cell is **not** osmotically balanced.

Osmotically Balanced Cell **Turgid Cell**
(not osmotically balanced)

Starch, however, is an **insoluble chemical** so it does not alter the osmotic balance within a cell. This makes starch a better storage molecule than glucose. The starch is stored in the cells in the form of **starch grains**.

Limiting Factors for Photosynthesis

There are several factors that can interact to limit the rate of photosynthesis:

- Temperature.
- Carbon dioxide concentration.
- Light intensity.

Any one of these factors, at a particular time, may be the limiting factor.

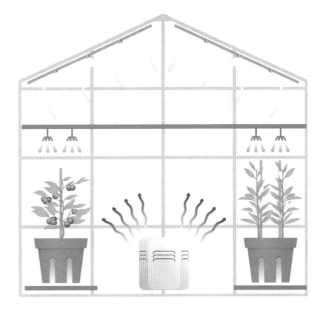

Temperature

1 As the temperature rises, so does the rate of photosynthesis. So, temperature is limiting the rate of photosynthesis.

2 As the temperature approaches 45°C, the enzymes controlling photosynthesis start to be destroyed and the rate of photosynthesis drops to zero.

Carbon Dioxide Concentration

1 As the carbon dioxide concentration rises, so does the rate of photosynthesis. So, carbon dioxide is limiting the rate of photosynthesis.

2 A rise in carbon dioxide levels now has no effect. Carbon dioxide is no longer the limiting factor. It must be either light or temperature.

Light Intensity

1 As the light intensity increases, so does the rate of photosynthesis. So, light intensity is limiting the rate of photosynthesis.

2 A rise in temperature now has no effect. Light intensity is no longer the limiting factor. It must be either carbon dioxide or temperature.

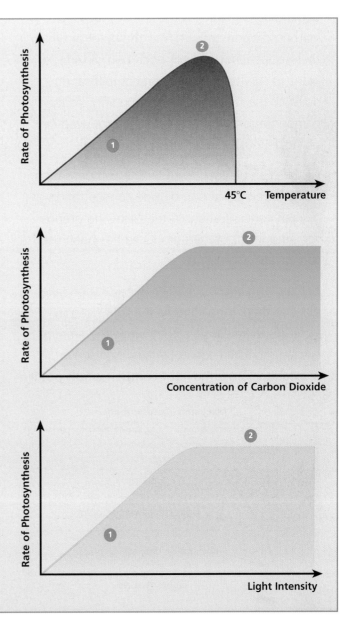

Further Biology

The Compensation Point

Photosynthesis in green plants only takes place during daylight hours. During a 24-hour period there is a point at which the **rate of photosynthesis** exactly **matches** the **rate of respiration**. This means that…

- the amount of carbon dioxide used in photosynthesis exactly matches the amount produced in respiration
- the amount of oxygen produced in photosynthesis exactly matches the amount used in respiration at that point in time.

This is called the **compensation point** and, depending on which is the limiting factor (carbon dioxide or light), it is the point at which there is just enough light or carbon dioxide for a plant to survive, (i.e. the light compensation point or the CO_2 compensation point). At the compensation point, all the food produced by photosynthesis is used up in respiration.

Graphs can be used to show the compensation point for either carbon dioxide concentration or oxygen concentration. In the following graphs, the amount of oxygen produced has been used to indicate photosynthesis.

In the graph below, initially only respiration takes place as there is no light. As the light intensity increases there comes a point when the amount of oxygen produced equals the amount used in respiration. This is the **light compensation point**.

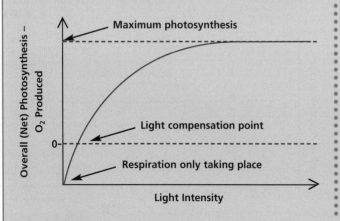

In the graph below, as the carbon dioxide concentration increases there comes a point where the amount of oxygen produced equals the amount used in respiration. This is the **carbon dioxide compensation point**.

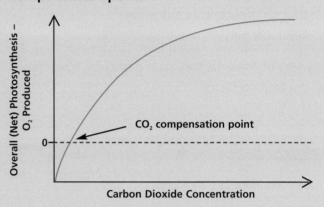

Over a 24-hour period, the level of photosynthesis can be plotted and analysed to identify the processes taking place. The graph below can be interpreted to give information about the rate of photosynthesis and respiration.

During the night photosynthesis stops, but respiration still takes place. Therefore, the net amount of carbon dioxide produced is high, and oxygen that is being used in respiration drops.

During the day, respiration continues and photosynthesis also takes place. Net carbon dioxide released is low and oxygen released is high. The compensation point is where both lines cross.

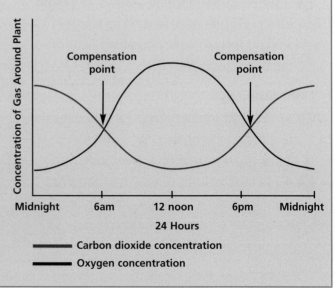

Limitations Measuring Photosynthesis

Accurate measurements of the rate of photosynthesis can be hard to achieve because it is difficult to measure a product of photosynthesis without altering one of the limiting factors (see p.65).

Other factors that affect photosynthesis are also difficult to control, e.g. wind and moisture levels.

Measurements, therefore, give an **indication** of the rate of photosynthesis rather than a **definitive rate**.

Carbon Dioxide Levels

One situation in which scientists have to make inferences upon data (and take into account other factors) is the debate over whether the activities of mankind are increasing the concentrations of atmospheric carbon dioxide.

The **Greenhouse Effect** means the Earth stays warmer than it would otherwise be. In February 2007, as part of the Intergovernmental Panel on Climate Change (IPCC), **over 2500** scientists from 130 countries unanimously agreed that the activities of man (e.g. burning fossil fuels and heavy industry) were most likely to be the cause of the increasing levels of carbon dioxide in the atmosphere, causing what is known as the **Enhanced Greenhouse Effect**.

It is believed that unless we lower the amount of carbon dioxide we produce, there is a 90% certainty that the Earth will be fundamentally changed forever. If nothing is done, by 2100, the Earth's temperature will have increased by 6.5°C. This increase will cause…

- the polar ice caps to melt
- sea levels to rise, which will flood low-level countries
- the extinction of entire species, such as polar bears.

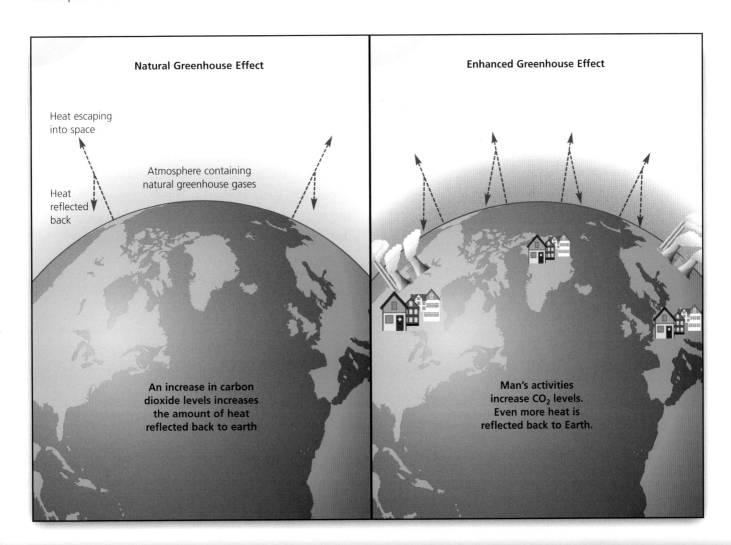

Natural Greenhouse Effect

Heat escaping into space

Atmosphere containing natural greenhouse gases

Heat reflected back

An increase in carbon dioxide levels increases the amount of heat reflected back to earth

Enhanced Greenhouse Effect

Man's activities increase CO$_2$ levels. Even more heat is reflected back to Earth.

Further Biology

Symbiosis

Symbiosis is a general term for a relationship in which members of different species live in close association with one another. The relationships can be…

- beneficial to both organisms
- beneficial to one organism, and neither harmful nor beneficial to the other
- beneficial to one organism and harmful to the other.

In the exam you will need to be able to recognise when a relationship is **symbiotic**, and the type of symbiosis involved.

To do this you need to look at each organism and decide which organism(s) benefit(s) from the relationship.

Mutualism

Mutualism is a symbiotic relationship from which both organisms benefit, for example, between clownfish and sea anemones.

The clownfish protects the anemone from anemone-eating fish, and in turn the stinging tentacles of the anemone protect the clownfish from its predators.

Commensalism

Commensalism is a symbiotic relationship which is beneficial to one organism, but does not harm or benefit the other, for example, between Remora fish and sharks.

Remora fish have suckers that can attach to larger fish, such as sharks. The fish benefit from the relationship because they are transported through the sea and feed off scraps of food surrounding the shark. The shark gains no benefit or harm from the relationship.

Parasitism

Parasitism is a symbiotic relationship that is beneficial to one organism (the **parasite**) and harmful to the other (the **host**). The parasite feeds off the host, but the host receives no benefit, in fact it is harmed. A parasite cannot survive without its host.

Two examples of parasites are tapeworms and leeches.

Beef Tapeworm

Tapeworms are caught by eating undercooked beef from cows that have eaten grass contaminated with human faeces. Once taken inside the human body, tapeworms live inside the intestines of the host (the human), absorbing the food that the host eats.

The shape and features of the tapeworm are adapted for its function. The top of the tapeworm has suckers and teeth-like structures to latch onto the inside of the host's intestine. Tapeworms are flat and very long (can be up to 10–15m) so they have a large surface area through which to line the intestine and absorb food.

Leeches

Leeches often live in freshwater streams. When a mammal enters the stream, leeches can detect the mammal's body heat. The leeches will quickly attach to the skin's surface of the host and start sucking the organism's blood.

A leech has a sucker at each end of its body. One sucker enables the leech to attach firmly to the host, whilst the other has teeth which enables the leech to suck the blood from the host. A leech also excretes an anticoagulant which stops the host's blood from clotting as it feeds.

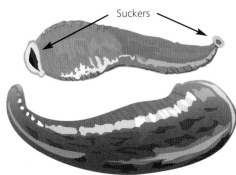

Suckers

The Importance of Understanding Parasites

Parasites can cause a large number of problems for humans. For example…

- they cause diseases, e.g. malaria
- they can have a big impact on food production (both from plants and animals) as a parasite can reduce the amount of food that can be harvested.

A parasite's body is specifically adapted to survive within a particular host, therefore, the **evolution** of the parasite is thought to be closely linked to that of the host. By understanding how parasites work, their life cycles and their needs, scientists can develop ways to stop them causing harm.

Malaria

Malaria is a disease carried by a parasite, which can lead to fever, anaemia, organ damage and death. Between 1 to 3 million people die from malaria every year and it is now mainly confined to Africa, Asia and Latin America. The disease is transmitted from person to person by the female mosquito. The disease progressively breaks down the body's red blood cells.

Plasmodium develop in the gut of the mosquito and are then passed on in the saliva of an infected insect each time it takes a new blood meal from a host. The parasites are then carried by the blood to the victim's liver where they invade the cells and multiply.

The life cycle of Plasmodium has evolved to be closely linked to the host. By understanding the life cycle, drugs can be developed to reduce the symptoms of the disease and programmes can be developed to destroy the wetland areas where mosquitoes breed.

Further Biology

HT Sickle-Cell Anaemia

Sickle-cell anaemia is a **hereditary blood disorder** that affects **haemoglobin** (the protein found in red blood cells that helps carry oxygen through the body).

It occurs when a person inherits two faulty **recessive genes** (one from each parent) which cause their red blood cells to change shape.

Normal red blood cells (with haemoglobin HbA) are flexible, round and move easily through the bloodstream, delivering oxygen to all the cells of the body for respiration.

Sickle-cell anaemia occurs when an abnormal form of haemoglobin (HbS) is produced. The red blood cells become sticky, stiff and fragile, and alternate between being round and being sickled-shaped until eventually they become sickle-shaped permanently.

These deformed blood cells block blood vessels and deprive the body's tissues and organs of oxygen.

Therefore, a sufferer will be anaemic, feel weak and tired and have very painful cramps throughout their body. They may also have eyesight problems and have random, intense joint pain.

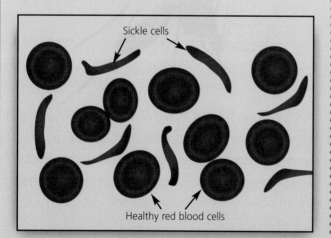
Sickle cells

Healthy red blood cells

Advantages of Being a Carrier

If a person inherits **two** faulty alleles they will have the disorder. If a person inherits just **one** faulty allele, they will be a **carrier** and may exhibit sickle-cell traits, i.e. they will have few symptoms but might have slight sickle-cell forms in their blood.

If a carrier reproduces with another carrier, there is a 25% chance that they will pass on full sickle-cell anaemia to their offspring.

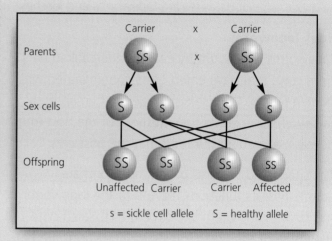
Carrier   x   Carrier

Parents   Ss   x   Ss

Sex cells   S   S   S   S

Offspring   SS   Ss   Ss   ss
              Unaffected Carrier   Carrier Affected

s = sickle cell allele   S = healthy allele

However, being a carrier for the sickle-cell allele can be an advantage in areas where malaria is common. Sickle cells are not infected by malaria parasites, therefore, a carrier is more likely to recover from an acute attack of malaria than a non-carrier.

Natural Selection

Malaria can kill or incapacitate people who have normal, healthy haemoglobin in their blood. Therefore, the number of people with normal haemoglobin in the population will decrease. Similarly, a person who inherits two sickle-cell alleles is less likely to be able to reproduce and pass on their genes.

However, if a person inherits just one sickle-cell allele, they will suffer few sickle-cell symptoms **and** are more likely to survive an attack of malaria. So these carriers are more likely to reproduce and pass their genes onto their offspring. Therefore, the number of people carrying the faulty gene will increase. This means that the frequency of the sickle-cell allele is higher than it would be if malaria did not exist. This is an example of **natural selection** in action (see p.25).

The Structure of Bacteria

Bacteria have…
- a cell wall (which gives a shape to the bacterium)
- a cell membrane (to allow substances to enter and leave the cell)
- DNA that appears to retain a circular shape. (The DNA is **not** in a nucleus.)

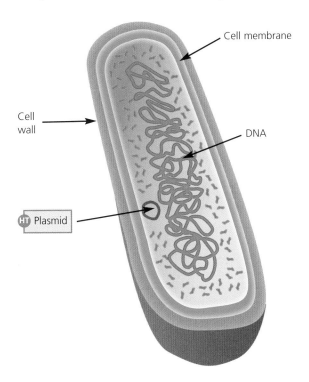

Cell membrane

Cell wall

DNA

HT Plasmid

> **HT** Bacteria also have **plasmids** which are made up of circular, double-stranded DNA. Plasmids are unique to bacteria. They can be copied, and move between different bacteria in a population. This means that resistance to certain antibiotics can be passed on without the bacteria reproducing.

Fermentation

A **fermenter** is a **controlled environment** that provides ideal conditions for microorganisms to live in, feed and produce the proteins needed. It allows the continuous culture of large quantities of microorganisms or their products, e.g. industrial quantities of **antibiotics** (by growing specially selected varieties of fungi that naturally produce the required antibiotic).

Fermenters can also be used to…
- **grow single-cell proteins**, for example mycoprotein (the main ingredient of Quorn™, a meat substitute for vegetarians)
- **culture enzymes** that can then be used in food production, for example rennin, which is used in cheese making and would otherwise have to be harvested from sheeps' stomachs.

Genetic Modification

DNA is the genetic material of all organisms and it contains the genes that code for the particular proteins that an organism needs. Proteins produced by one organism may not be produced by another.

By carrying out genetic modification, the gene that produces a desirable protein can be inserted into another organism so that it too produces the required protein.

This is achieved by selecting and **isolating** the desired gene. Once isolated, the gene is **replicated** (copied exactly and increased in number) before being **inserted / transferred** into the target organism.

Further Biology

Using a Vector

The desired gene is inserted into the target bacterium using a **vector**. The vector used could be a **virus** or a **plasmid**.

1. Viruses spread easily into cells so they are ideally adapted for passing on DNA. If the desired gene is very large it can be inserted into a virus that infects bacteria (called bacteriophages).

   The bacteriophage will, in turn, infect and pass on the DNA into a bacterium. The bacterium will then reproduce and make the product from the desired gene.

2. Plasmids can be replicated very easily and rapidly spread through a bacterial population.

   The plasmid is cut open and the gene is inserted (a gene for antibiotic resistance is also inserted). The plasmids spread amongst the bacterial population.

   An antibiotic is used to identify the plasmids carrying the desired gene (as they do not die from the antibiotic). The surviving population produces the gene product, which can then be harvested.

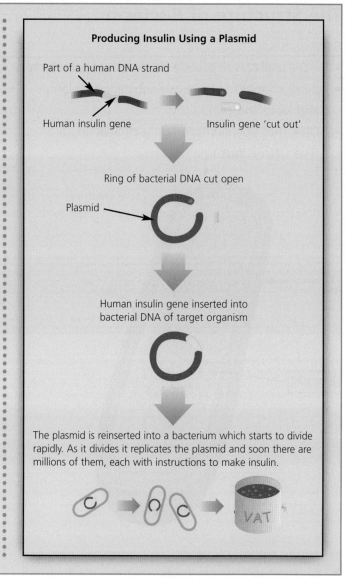

Producing Insulin Using a Plasmid

Part of a human DNA strand

Human insulin gene

Insulin gene 'cut out'

Ring of bacterial DNA cut open

Plasmid

Human insulin gene inserted into bacterial DNA of target organism

The plasmid is reinserted into a bacterium which starts to divide rapidly. As it divides it replicates the plasmid and soon there are millions of them, each with instructions to make insulin.

VAT

Using Genetic Modification

Genetic modification is now used to create an increasing number of drugs and hormones to treat patients.

For example, genetically modified microorganisms are used in the production of insulin for people who have diabetes. Millions of people worldwide lack the ability to produce insulin so they require regular injections of insulin.

Until recently, the insulin was taken from pigs and cows. However, it is now possible to use genetically modified bacteria to produce human insulin.

Genetic modification can also be used when growing crops. Farmers often have to deal with different diseases, which can reduce crop yield. Genetic modification can be used to transfer genes for disease resistance from another plant into the crop so that the crop will be affected less by the disease.

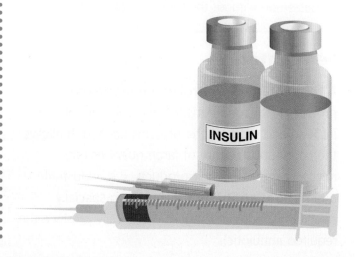

INSULIN

Advantages and Disadvantages of Genetic Modification

Genetic modification has the potential to solve many problems for society. For example, it can be used…

- to produce healthier crops which can produce greater yields
- to reduce the need for pesticides which cause pollution
- to enable some crops (e.g. bananas) to naturally carry vaccines so they would not need to be kept refrigerated
- to allow organizations to monitor the release and spread of genetically modified crops by looking for antibiotic-resistant markers in crops. (The markers will only be there if the crop has been modified.)
- to enable some drugs (e.g. insulin) to be made from human, rather than animal, DNA.

However there are also drawbacks. For example…
- genetically modified organisms may be expensive
- there may be unknown effects on ecosystems
- crops that have been modified may pass the genes on to other non-modified crops and weeds. This would lead to resistance in weeds and the need to use more pesticides on crops
- the antibiotic resistance may itself be passed on
- some people ethically disagree with the technology and will not buy genetically modified products.

All these issues have to be considered and any decision has to be based on balancing the potential benefits against potential risks. Decisions in the UK are taken by DEFRA (Department for Environment, Food and Rural Affairs).

Genetic Testing

Since the discovery of the structure of DNA in 1952, the understanding of DNA has led to technology that can be used in genetic testing, for example…

- establishing paternity
- determining whether a gene causing a genetic disorder is carried by the patient.

A gene can be tested using the following method:

1. DNA is isolated from white blood cells (which, unlike red blood cells, have a nucleus). The DNA is often amplified at this stage so that there is enough material to experiment with. It is then broken up into different sized pieces.

2. In the meantime, a gene probe is created. This is a single-stranded DNA or RNA sequence that has bases (adenine, thymine, guanine and cytosine) that will pair up with the complementary bases on the target gene. The probe will only attach if the desired gene is present in a sample.

3. The probe has a marker attached, which causes it to fluoresce when UV light is shone onto it. (This indicates that the person being tested has the disorder.)

Alternatively, the probe may have a radioisotope, which emits radioactive particles that can be detected by X-ray film. When detected, it indicates that the person has a copy of the gene in question. This process is called **autoradiography**.

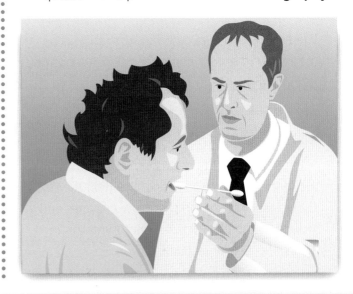

Further Biology

Healthy Ranges

There is no 'normal' value for factors such as heart rate and blood pressure. People differ in a wide variety of ways, e.g. different weights and different metabolisms.

So, instead of setting values for a healthy heart rate or blood pressure, a **range** is given. However, even with this set range, someone may fall outside the range and still be healthy.

Respiration

Respiration is the **release of energy** from food chemicals. There are two types of respiration:
- Aerobic respiration.
- Anaerobic respiration.

Aerobic Respiration

Aerobic respiration releases energy through the breakdown of glucose molecules, by combining them with **oxygen** inside living cells. The majority of organisms respire aerobically and it is the main method of releasing energy from food chemicals.

In humans the aerobic respiration equation is as follows:

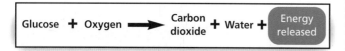

Glucose + Oxygen → Carbon dioxide + Water + Energy released

HT ATP Production

The energy that is released in respiration is used to synthesise a chemical called Adenosine triphosphate (ATP).

ATP is a chemical that is often referred to as being the '**energy currency**' of living things.

ATP transfers energy from chemical bonds to the reactions that require energy within the cell. These reactions are used by many enzymes and include metabolic reactions, photosynthesis in plants and cellular respiration.

Muscles

Muscles are made up of tissues that contract and relax. When the muscles in an organism are working, they need more energy than when they are at rest. The energy to contract comes from respiration.

> **HT** The energy to contract specifically comes from the chemical **ATP**.

N.B. Muscle fibres exist in groups, and these groups are surrounded by a protective membrane.

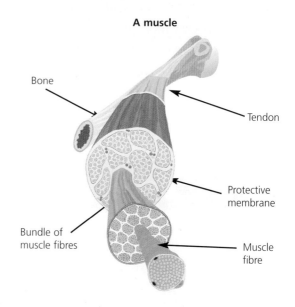

A muscle

Bone

Tendon

Protective membrane

Bundle of muscle fibres

Muscle fibre

During Exercise

During exercise, muscles require a faster supply of glucose and oxygen. These substances are transported to the muscles via blood. Respiration increases and, due to the increase in glucose and oxygen, the muscles are able to move and work faster.

The faster rate of respiration also produces more carbon dioxide as a waste product. Therefore, more blood needs to be pumped around the body to remove the carbon dioxide, so the heart rate will increase. The breathing rate will also increase to ensure that there is enough oxygen circulating round the body in the blood cells.

Therefore, during exercise both the breathing rate and pulse rate increase.

Anaerobic Respiration

Anaerobic respiration takes place **without oxygen**. In humans the equation for anaerobic respiration is:

Glucose ⟶ Lactic acid **+** Energy released

If a person is exercising vigorously, (e.g. sprinting) not enough oxygen can get to the muscles so aerobic respiration cannot take place. Instead, anaerobic respiration occurs, which produces short bursts of energy.

Anaerobic respiration is less efficient, and produces less energy than aerobic respiration. It also produces **lactic acid**, which builds up in the muscle cells. This means that the body cannot use anaerobic respiration to produce energy for long periods of time.

Oxygen Debt

Lactic acid is toxic and can cause harm to muscle cells if it is not removed. After anaerobic respiration has stopped, the lactic acid needs to be broken back down into carbon dioxide and water, which can then be removed from muscle cells via the blood.

Therefore, after vigorous exercise there is a time period before the body can return to normal functions. Extra oxygen is needed to break down the lactic acid – this is called the **oxygen debt**.

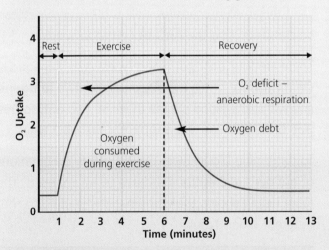

Advantage of Anaerobic Respiration

Aerobic respiration releases more energy per glucose molecule than anaerobic respiration:

- Aerobic respiration produces 32 ATP per glucose molecule.
- Anaerobic respiration produces 2 ATP per glucose molecule.

Although the amount of energy released from anaerobic respiration is comparatively low, there are advantages to using this type of respiration.

In evolutionary terms, being able to respire with low levels of oxygen is an advantage when escaping from danger, e.g. a predator.

The extra few seconds where a human can continue to run could mean the difference between life and death.

This advantage is also relevant for other organisms.

After aerobic respiration stops, anaerobic respiration gives the man the extra energy needed to escape from the bull.

Further Biology

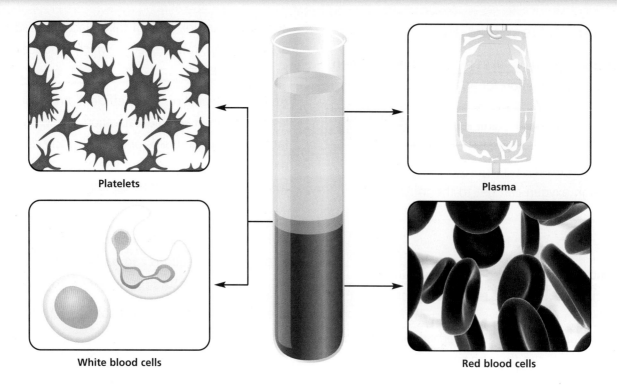

Platelets

White blood cells

Plasma

Red blood cells

Blood

Blood has four components.

Plasma is a straw-coloured liquid that transports…
- carbon dioxide from the organs to the lungs
- the soluble products of digestion from the small intestines to the organs
- urea from the liver to the kidneys.

Red blood cells transport oxygen from the lungs to the organs. They have no nucleus and are packed with haemoglobin, a red pigment that binds with oxygen. Their bi-concave shape provides a bigger surface area through which to absorb oxygen.

White blood cells have a nucleus and come in a variety of shapes. They fight infection and defend the body against microorganisms. Some white blood cells engulf and kill microorganisms. Others produce antibodies to attack microorganisms.

Platelets are tiny particles found in blood plasma. They are not cells and they do not have a nucleus. When a blood vessel is damaged, platelets clump together to form a meshwork of fibres in order to form a clot and prevent blood from leaving the body.

Blood Types

There are different ways of classifying blood. The most well known and medically important blood types are in the **ABO system**, discovered in 1901 by Karl Landsteiner. All humans (as well as other primates) can be classified using the ABO blood group system.

There are four principal blood types: A, B, AB and O. On the surface of the red blood cells are two **antigens**, and within the blood plasma there are two **antibodies** (see p.14) that are responsible for the ABO types.

To determine blood type, the different combinations of antigens and antibodies have to be analysed. The table below shows the combinations leading to the different blood types.

ABO Blood Type	Presence of Antigen or Antibody			
	Antigen A	Antigen B	Anti-A Antibody	Anti-B Antibody
A	Yes	No	No	Yes
B	No	Yes	Yes	No
O	No	No	Yes	Yes
AB	Yes	Yes	No	No

The ABO System

Landsteiner worked out the ABO system because he wanted to understand why some people died when receiving blood transfusions whilst others lived.

The discovery of blood types meant that blood transfusions could work successfully with people of different blood types.

In a blood transfusion…
*   the patient receiving blood is called the **recipient**
*   the person donating blood is called the **donor**.

It is very important that the **antigens** in the **donor's** blood are analysed to see if they will react with the **antibodies** in the **recipient's** blood. For example, if a donor whose blood contained anti-B antibodies is transfused into a recipient with antigen B, the recipient's blood would clot causing circulation problems and possibly death.

N.B. The presence of antibodies in the blood plasma only matters in the recipient's blood, not in the donor's blood. This is because the level of antibodies that come through a transfusion is very low and is not enough to clot blood.

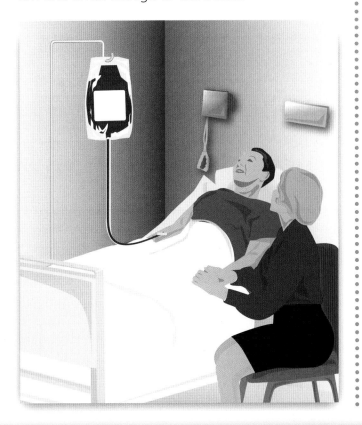

People with blood type O are **universal donors** because their blood type does not contain either antigen. However, because their blood carries both antibodies, they can only receive blood from donors who also have blood type O.

People with blood type AB are **universal recipients** because their blood contains both antigens and, therefore, it does not matter if the donated blood has all, or none, of the antigens.

To interpret compatibility data on blood types, you first need to identify the recipient's antibodies and then see if the donor has antigens that match the antibodies. In practice, it is a simple process.

For example, half of a blood sample is mixed with a serum containing anti-A antibodies, and the other half is mixed with a serum containing anti-B antibodies. Clotting indicates the ABO type, so if the blood sample clots by the anti-A antibody, but not the anti-B antibody, it means that antigen A is present but not antigen B. Therefore, the blood type is A.

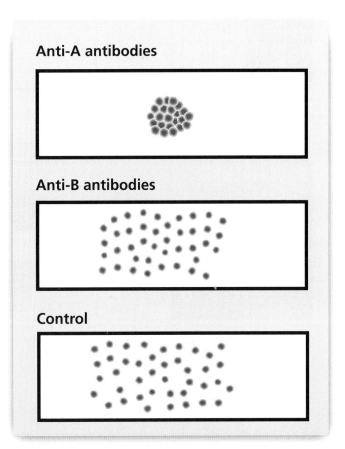

Anti-A antibodies

Anti-B antibodies

Control

Further Biology

Blood Group Genetics

Blood type is carried on a single gene on the ninth chromosome. It can have one of three alleles (matching the blood types), i.e. A, B or O.

Alleles A and B are **co-dominant**, which means that both antigens will be produced on the red blood cell if both alleles are present.

The O allele is recessive to both A and B, which means that blood type O will only be produced if neither A nor B is present.

Every child inherits one allele from their mother and one from their father. The table below illustrates the inheritance of the 4 different blood types.

Parent Alleles →	A	B	O
A	AA (A type)	AB (AB type)	AO (A type)
B	AB (AB type)	BB (B type)	BO (B type)
O	AO (A type)	BO (B type)	OO (O type)

Genetic diagrams can be drawn to illustrate the inheritance of ABO blood types.

		Father (A Alleles)	
		A	A
Mother (O Alleles)	O	AO (A type)	AO (A type)
	O	AO (A type)	AO (A type)

There is a 100% chance that offspring will have blood type A, but will carry the O allele.

		Father (AB Alleles)	
		A	B
Mother (O Alleles)	O	AO (A type)	BO (B type)
	O	AO (A type)	BO (B type)

There is a 50% chance that offspring will have blood type A and a 50% chance they will have blood type B. All offspring will carry the O allele.

		Father (AO Alleles)	
		A	O
Mother (B Alleles)	B	AB (AB type)	BO (B type)
	B	AB (AB type)	BO (B type)

There is a 50% chance that offspring will have blood type AB and a 50% chance they will have blood type B.

		Father (AB Alleles)	
		A	B
Mother (AB Alleles)	A	AA (A type)	AB (AB type)
	B	AB (AB type)	BB (B type)

There is a 50% chance that offspring will have blood type AB, 25% chance they will have blood type A and 25% chance they will have blood type B.

		Father (O Alleles)	
		O	O
Mother (O Alleles)	O	OO (O type)	OO (O type)
	O	OO (O type)	OO (O type)

There is a 100% chance that offspring will have blood type O.

The Heart

The heart is a muscular organ in the circulatory system that beats automatically, pumping blood around the body. The rate at which the heart beats will vary according to stress, exertion and disease.

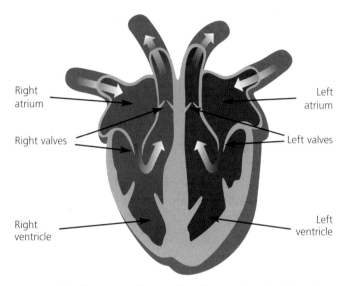

Right atrium

Left atrium

Right valves

Left valves

Right ventricle

Left ventricle

Most of the heart wall is made of muscle. The left side of the heart is more muscular than the right side because it pumps blood around the whole body, (whereas the right side pumps blood only to the lungs).

The heart has four chambers:
- Two **atria** which are the smaller, less muscular upper chambers that receive blood coming back to the heart from the veins.
- Two **ventricles** which are the larger, more muscular lower chambers.

Valves ensure that the blood flows in the right direction (i.e. not backwards).

When the heart muscles **relax**, blood flows into the atria through veins from the lungs and the rest of the body. The atria then **contract**, squeezing blood into ventricles.

When the ventricles **contract**, blood is forced out of the lower chambers which carry the blood to the body and lungs. The heart then **relaxes** and the whole process starts again.

Blood entering the heart via the right atrium has travelled around the body and is deoxygenated. It is pumped into the lungs where the haemoglobin binds to the oxygen, becoming **oxyhaemoglobin**. The oxygen-rich blood returns to the heart via the left atrium and is then pumped to the rest of the body.

The blood returns to the heart twice on every circuit of the body. This type of circulation system is called **double circulation**.

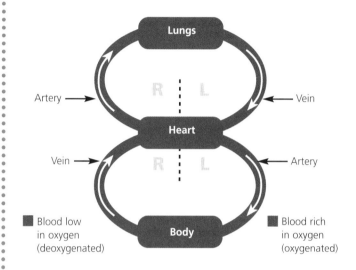

Lungs

Artery

Vein

R | L

Heart

Vein

Artery

R | L

Body

■ Blood low in oxygen (deoxygenated)

■ Blood rich in oxygen (oxygenated)

Blood Vessels

There are three types of blood vessel:
- **Arteries** carry blood away from the heart towards the organs. They have thick, elastic walls to cope with the high pressure of blood coming from the heart. Substances cannot pass through the artery walls.
- **Veins** carry blood from the organs back to the heart. They have thinner, less elastic walls and they contain valves to prevent the blood flowing backwards. Substances cannot pass through the vein walls.
- **Capillaries** connect arteries to the veins. They have a narrow, thin wall that is only one cell thick. The exchange of substances between cells and the blood takes place here.

Artery　　　Vein　　　Valve　　　Capillary

Further Biology

Tissue Fluid

The plasma of arterial blood contains the dissolved products from digestion. Around the body tissues are networks of capillaries called **capillary beds**. The flow of blood in the capillary beds is very slow so plasma leaves and becomes **tissue fluid**. Tissue fluid enables the nutrients required by the cells (e.g. glucose needed for respiration, oxygen and hormones) to diffuse into the tissue cells.

The tissue fluid also collects and carries away some cellular waste products, such as carbon dioxide (waste product from respiration) and urea. The majority of the tissue fluid (90%) returns to the capillary bed where it again becomes plasma and continues its journey through the body, this time in the veins.

The Skeletal System

All animals can be divided into two groups based on whether they have a backbone (**vertebrates**) or not (**invertebrates**).

Vertebrates have an internal skeleton that has the following functions:
- **Support**, e.g. legs and spine to stand upright.
- **Movement**, e.g. legs to walk.
- **Protection** of internal organs, e.g. skull to protect the brain.

Bones, Muscles, Ligaments and Tendons

Bones are rigid tissues that make up the skeleton.

Muscle is tissue designed to contract and relax.

Ligaments are tough, fibrous, elastic connective tissues that connect **bone** joints together in a joint.

Tendons are tough, fibrous, elastic connective tissues that connect **muscle to bone** or **muscle to muscle**.

Bones, muscles, tendons and ligaments combine to enable joints to move easily and carry out work.

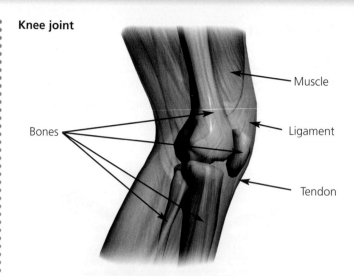

Knee joint

Muscle

Ligament

Bones

Tendon

Joint Movement

Muscles can only move bones by **contracting**. So they work in **antagonistic pairs**, i.e. one muscle contracts whilst another muscle relaxes.

For example…
- to lift the lower arm, the biceps contracts and the triceps relaxes.
- to lower the arm, the triceps contracts and the biceps relaxes.

If the tendon connecting the triceps to the bone were cut, the triceps would not be able to contract and the arm would remain in the up position.

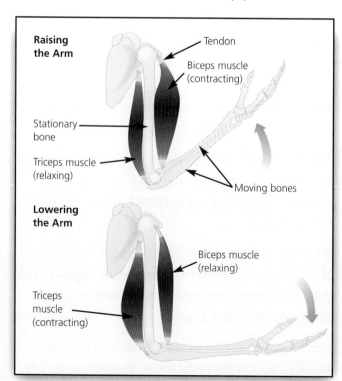

Raising the Arm

Tendon

Biceps muscle (contracting)

Stationary bone

Triceps muscle (relaxing)

Moving bones

Lowering the Arm

Biceps muscle (relaxing)

Triceps muscle (contracting)

Cartilage and Synovial Fluid

Joints are covered by a smooth layer of **cartilage**. Cartilage is a tough connective tissue that helps reduce wear and tear by preventing the bones of the joint from rubbing together.

Synovial fluid is an oily fluid with an egg-like consistency, which enables the joint to move freely by reducing friction and cushioning the joint against bumps and knocks.

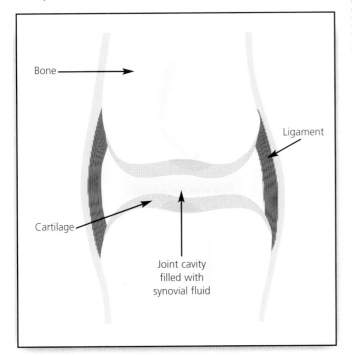

Medical History Assessment

Practitioners are people with special scientific or medical training. They help people to maintain and improve their health and fitness. Some examples of practitioners are doctors, nurses and fitness instructors.

A patient's medical or lifestyle history needs to be disclosed before the start of any treatment or exercise programme. This ensures that any treatment suggested for the patient is effective and will not make the problem worse or trigger another problem.

The following are all factors that a practitioner needs to be made aware of.

Symptoms – visible or noticeable effects on the body, which can be used to identify a problem.

Current medication – different medicines can sometimes conflict with one another (i.e. cancel each other out or have a harmful or enhanced effect on the body if they are combined).

Alcohol consumption – high levels of alcohol consumed regularly can cause physical problems, e.g. obesity and damage to the kidneys and liver. Some medicines can react badly if taken with alcohol.

Tobacco consumption – smoking can lead to many disorders and diseases, e.g. lung cancer, bronchitis, emphysema, and a higher risk of developing heart disease and high blood pressure.

Level of physical activity – the more exercise a person takes the healthier they will be. Lack of exercise can lead to depression, anxiety, obesity, tiredness, weak bones and problems with sleeping and concentration.

Family medical history – some medical conditions can be genetic (inherited), therefore, it is important to know a patient's family history as there may be other family members who have had the same condition and treatment for it.

Previous treatments – a patient returning with the same symptoms might require a different diagnosis or need to be sent to a specialist for further investigation.

Further Biology

Patient Assessment

A patient must be properly assessed before any diagnostic tests are carried out, to ensure that the test will not make the patient's condition worse.

The risk of carrying out the test or procedure must be assessed and balanced against the chances of being able to cure or reduce the symptoms.

For example, if a patient has a suspected peanut allergy, it would be very dangerous to ask the patient to eat a peanut to test for the allergy. There are other, less life-threatening tests that can be carried out instead.

For example, a scratch test, where tiny nut traces are placed on the patient's skin in a droplet of water. A sterile needle is then used to scratch the skin through the liquid drop. If the skin reddens and blisters around the scratch, it indicates that the patient is allergic to nuts.

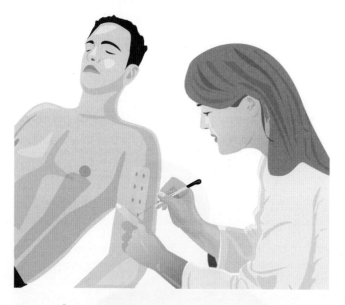

Regular Contact

Regular contact between a patient / client and a practitioner has many benefits.

The practitioner has the opportunity to become more familiar with the medical history and background of the patient, and the patient will feel more comfortable and reassured if they see the same practitioner each time.

Recording Information

A person's medical or fitness information must be recorded, stored and made available to other people on the practitioner's team. This is for the patient's benefit – if the practitioner is unavailable then another practitioner can read the patient's notes and continue the treatment without having to start the diagnosis from the beginning.

It is also important to store information in case anything happens to the patient in the future. If necessary, records can be checked to see if there were errors in diagnosis so that procedures can be changed. In the very rare cases that a practitioner does not follow procedures, the records can then be used as evidence to prosecute.

After the Diagnosis

Depending on the diagnosis, there are a number of different treatments or methods that could be used to improve health or fitness.

All treatments carry some risk, for example, a treatment could cause further harm or have side effects. The practitioner has to weigh the known risks against the benefits gained. Drugs in the United Kingdom are required by law to state all known side effects.

Before a patient is given or undertakes a treatment, the practitioner needs to obtain his or her consent (their agreement) to go through with the procedure. The patient must be made aware of the risks and likelihood of success so that they can make an informed decision before consenting.

There is often more than one way to achieve an agreed target. For example, it might be that greater levels of fitness could solve the problem or cure an illness. Sometimes a period of recovery is needed to return to normal. In other cases, rehabilitation might be needed, e.g. learning how to walk again after an accident.

Physiotherapy

A physiotherapist specialises in the treatment of skeletal-muscular injuries. Physiotherapists understand how the body works and can help patients re-train or re-use a part of their body that is not functioning properly. This is normally achieved with various exercises to strengthen muscles that have become weakened.

There are many different exercises and it is the physiotherapist's job to choose the best course of treatment for each patient.

For example, an injured leg could be treated by following the exercise programme below:

- Warming up the joint by riding a stationary exercise bicycle, then straightening and raising the leg.
- Extending the leg while sitting (a weight may be worn on the ankle for this exercise).
- Raising the leg while lying on the stomach.
- Exercising in a pool (walking as fast as possible in chest-deep water, performing small flutter kicks while holding onto the side of the pool, and raising each leg to 90° in chest-deep water while pressing the back against the side of the pool).

Monitoring and Assessing Progress

A treatment or fitness training programme needs to be monitored to check that it is having the desired effect. It can then be modified depending on the patient's progress. For example, a programme might be modified before completion if...

- the patient is finding the programme **too hard** (the problem could continue or a new injury could occur)
- the patient is finding the programme **too easy** (progress would be slow and the patient might not recover fast enough).

One way of monitoring progress during training is to measure the **pulse rate** or **aerobic fitness** of a patient / client. A patient who is increasing his / her aerobic fitness should lower his / her heart rate and have a faster recovery rate.

After treatment or training is complete, the patient can be called back for a check-up. Questions about progress and issues are asked and sometimes tests are carried out, e.g. the pulse rate might be checked.

HT Recording Progress

It is essential that accurate records are kept during treatment or fitness training because the records can be used to assess progress and determine trends. Inaccurate records could slow down progress or even make a condition worse.

However, progress records need to take into account the accuracy and reliability of the recording techniques.

For example, if a person is dieting they would normally weigh themselves on a regular basis, maybe every day. However, it is usual for water levels in the body to fluctuate, which can affect body weight. Measuring weight once or twice a week is a more accurate way to determine the sustained effects of a diet.

Further Biology

Injuries Caused by Excessive Exercise

The human body can withstand a lot of exercise. However, **excessive exercise** (over-exertion or not being properly prepared for exercise) can put the body under a lot of strain, which can lead to injuries. Injuries include sprains, dislocations and torn ligaments or tendons.

Sprains

A **sprain** is where an activity causes a stretch in a **ligament**. Ankles, knees and wrists are very vulnerable to sprains.

*   A sprained ankle can occur when the foot turns inward because this puts extreme tension on the ligaments of the outer ankle.
*   A sprained knee can be the result of a sudden twist.
*   A wrist can be sprained by falling on an outstretched hand.

The **symptoms** of sprains include…

*   **swelling**, due to fluid building up at the site of the sprain
*   **pain** – the joint hurts and may throb. The pain can increase if the injured part / area is pressed, moved in certain directions (depending on the ligament), or if weight is put on it.
*   **redness** and **warmth**, caused by increased blood flow to the injured area.

Treatment for a sprain is in the form of **RICE**:

*   **Rest** – the patient should rest and not move the injured part of the body.
*   **Ice** – should be placed on the injured part for short periods (wrapped in suitable fabric to prevent ice burns) to reduce swelling and bleeding.
*   **Compression** – gentle pressure should be applied with a bandage to reduce the build up of fluid that causes swelling.
*   **Elevation** – the injured body part should be raised (to reduce blood pressure, which would then lead to less blood flow and swelling).

Torn Ligaments and Tendons

A particularly **severe sprain** could mean that a ligament has been torn. Tendons can also be torn.

A torn ligament or tendon is painful and takes a long time to heal. The blood supply to ligaments is poor, compared to that for other parts of the body, so the materials needed for repair will be slower to arrive. A further consequence is that the bones connected to the ligament may not be in the correct position. Surgery may be required if the ligament is badly torn.

Dislocations

A sudden severe impact can cause certain joints to become **dislocated** (when two bones are no longer connected at the joint). This unusual position of the bones is very painful and could also result in torn ligaments and tendons. Dislocated joints can often be mistaken for broken bones because they produce similar pain, mis-shaped body parts and severe swelling.

The Exam Paper

One of the aims of OCR Twenty First Century Biology is to develop your knowledge and understanding of key scientific explanations and ideas, so that you can evaluate information about important science-based issues and make informed personal decisions when required.

In addition to your practical investigation and case study, you will have to sit three exams.

The first two papers will focus on the scientific explanations and ideas covered in Modules 1–3 and Modules 4–6 respectively (covered on pages 4–84 of this revision guide).

The third paper will cover Module 7, Further Biology, and also your understanding of Ideas in Context. The Idea in Context question(s) will be based on current science-based issues (which you may well be aware of from coverage in the media).

To answer these questions, you will have to recall scientific facts and draw upon your knowledge of how science works, i.e. the practices and procedures involved in collecting scientific evidence, and its impact on society.

This section of the revision guide looks in more detail at the Ideas in Context section of the Unit 3 exam. It looks at the type of questions that may come up, the format that they are likely to take, and what skills you will need to use to answer them.

You will sit either the Foundation or Higher Tier paper. This will be decided with your teacher during the build up to the exams.

Ideas in Context

Question Format

The Ideas in Context question will be based on a topic covered in Modules 1–6. Each year, the topic featured in the exam is chosen at random. You will not be asked a question relating to any topics that are not covered on the specification.

The pre-release material will be sent to your school before the exam. This material is presented as facts and information about a science-based issue connected to the chosen topic. This could be written information, data (i.e. tables and graphs), or a combination of both.

You will be able to read through the pre-release material in class and look up any technical terms or phrases that you do not understand. You are not expected to do further research, but you should revise any of the relevant scientific explanations or ideas.

In the exam you will be given a fresh copy of the pre-release material and a series of questions relating to the information.

You will **not** be able to take the original articles or any notes into the exam with you.

The questions can take a variety of formats, from multiple-choice and matching questions to data analysis and questions that require a written response. The questions will be designed to test your…

- understanding of the information
- understanding of related scientific information
- understanding of the practices and procedures used in scientific investigations
- ability to identify the benefits and drawbacks of the science and technology involved
- ability to identify the different arguments surrounding the issue (i.e. for and against)
- ability to evaluate the impact of the technology involved on the environment and society.

Exam and Revision Tips

- Try to watch the news and read newspapers and publications like *New Scientist* and *Flipside* whenever you can. This will alert you to any topical science-based issues that might come up in the exam. You should be able to find these in your school library or resource centre. You can also find websites for these publications with up-to-date information.

- Make sure that you read the information carefully before attempting to answer any of the questions. Underline key words as this might help you to focus on the content.

- The answers to many of the questions will be in the information, so keep referring back to it.

- The total marks available for each question are shown in the right-hand margin. The marks allocated and the space provided should give you a clue as to the length of answer required and how much information you need to give. For example, if a question is worth two marks, the examiner is likely to be looking for two key points in your answer.

- If you are asked to make a calculation, always show your working. Marks are often given if you use the correct method, even if the final answer is incorrect.

- If you are giving measurements, make sure you remember to include the units of measure and use the correct abbreviation.

- For some questions, an extra mark might be awarded for the quality of written communication of your answer. If this is the case, it will say so clearly by the relevant question and a pencil icon (✎) will be shown. This means that you should…
    - write in clear sentences
    - order your sentences in a logical way
    - pay special attention to your spelling, punctuation and grammar
    - use the correct scientific words.

The next few pages include an exam-style question, with model answers and handy hints on how to approach the different parts of the question.

Ideas in Context

The information below is based on the content in Module B4: Homeostasis. Make sure you read all the information below carefully before you even attempt to answer the questions.

1

Answer all questions.

Question 1

Homeostasis is the process whereby the body prevents the outside environment from changing things inside the body.

It is important that the body stays at 37°C and keeps the same level of water in the blood no matter what is happening outside the body.

Read the following article about what happens to the human body when mountaineers attempt to climb Mount Everest.

INTO THE DEATH ZONE

Climbers call mountains over 26000 feet, the death zone. Mount Everest is 29035 feet high. Over 90 climbers have climbed Mount Everest.

Climbers can suffer from frostbite, when fingers and toes freeze. They also have to survive winds of over 90 miles per hour. Above 25000 feet, the air is so dry, that climbers can breathe out 5 litres of water in their breath every day.

Ultraviolet radiation increases by 4% for every thousand feet and Everest is over 29000 feet high. These levels of ultraviolet radiation can cause blindness.

The following data show what happens to the body at higher altitudes.

29000 feet
Air pressure 30%.
Climber may hallucinate.
Resting heart rate 123 beats per minute.

18000 feet
Air pressure 50%.
No one on Earth has a home above this height.
Lungs breathe out too much carbon dioxide turning blood alkaline.
Kidneys excrete more water.

9000 feet
Air pressure 75%.
People get out of breath.
People get headaches as brain starts to swell.
Body starts to make more red blood cells.
Resting heart rate 85 beats per minute.

Specimen paper: Additional Science A

Reproduced from an OCR specimen exam paper

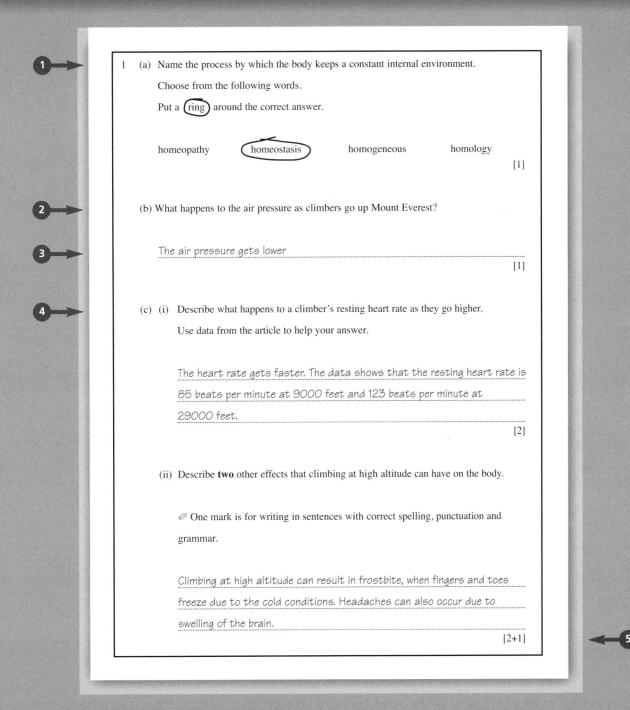

1   (a)   Name the process by which the body keeps a constant internal environment.

Choose from the following words.

Put a ⟨ring⟩ around the correct answer.

homeopathy   ⟨homeostasis⟩   homogeneous   homology

[1]

(b) What happens to the air pressure as climbers go up Mount Everest?

The air pressure gets lower

[1]

(c)   (i)   Describe what happens to a climber's resting heart rate as they go higher.

Use data from the article to help your answer.

The heart rate gets faster. The data shows that the resting heart rate is 85 beats per minute at 9000 feet and 123 beats per minute at 29000 feet.

[2]

(ii) Describe **two** other effects that climbing at high altitude can have on the body.

✏ One mark is for writing in sentences with correct spelling, punctuation and grammar.

Climbing at high altitude can result in frostbite, when fingers and toes freeze due to the cold conditions. Headaches can also occur due to swelling of the brain.

[2+1]

1 This is a multiple choice question. You can answer this correctly by referring back to the information. With a multiple choice question like this, even if you do not know it immediately, you can sometimes arrive at the correct answer by eliminating the wrong answers one at a time.

2 This part of the question is testing how carefully you have read the information. The answer is in the text, but you might have missed it if you were skim-reading.

3 Your answer does not have to be word perfect; there are several different wordings that are acceptable as an answer here, i.e. gets less / lower / drops. The most important thing is that your answer clearly states that air pressure is decreasing.

4 Read the question carefully – there are two parts to this question. You must describe what happens to a climber's resting heart rate AND include relevant data from the article to support your answer to get full marks.

5 This question is worth two marks, one for each correct effect you describe. The pencil symbol (✏) means that an extra mark is available for a clear, well ordered answer.

To earn this extra mark, make sure you write in clear sentences and order them in a logical way. Finally, make sure your spelling, punctuation and grammar are all correct.

Ideas in Context

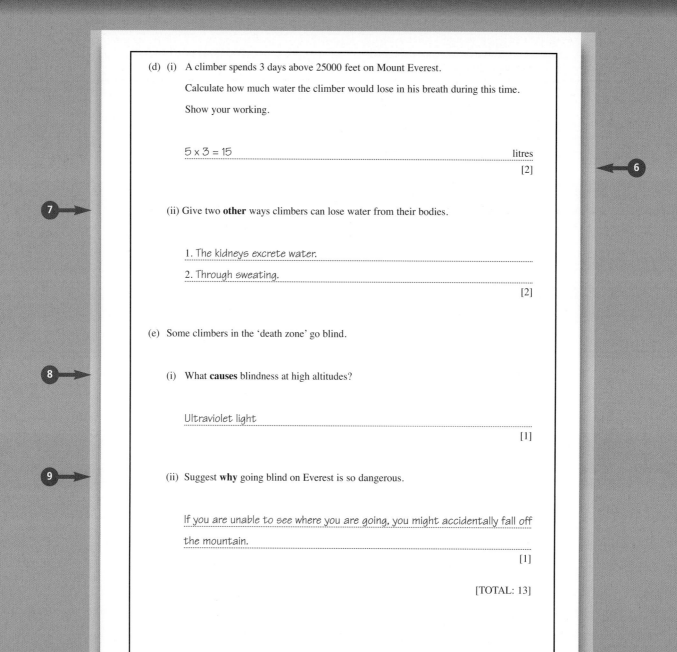

(d) (i) A climber spends 3 days above 25000 feet on Mount Everest.

Calculate how much water the climber would lose in his breath during this time.

Show your working.

5 x 3 = 15 .... litres

[2]

6

(ii) Give two **other** ways climbers can lose water from their bodies.

1. The kidneys excrete water.

2. Through sweating.

[2]

7

(e) Some climbers in the 'death zone' go blind.

(i) What **causes** blindness at high altitudes?

Ultraviolet light

[1]

8

(ii) Suggest **why** going blind on Everest is so dangerous.

If you are unable to see where you are going, you might accidentally fall off

the mountain.

[1]

9

[TOTAL: 13]

6 Look at the marks for each question (given on the right-hand side of the question paper) – they will give you a clue as to how much information you need to give. This question is worth two marks: one for the correct answer, and one for showing the working out. The amount of water lost through breathing each day is given in the text.

7 This question requires you to recall information from module B4, which is why it is important for you to revise thoroughly before the exam.

8 This question is testing your understanding of the information given. By referring back to the text you should find the answer in the third paragraph of the article.

9 This question is a bit harder than the rest, because the answer is not in the text or the specification. But do not be put off – it just requires a bit of careful thinking and common sense.

Adaptation – the gradual change of a particular organism over generations to become better suited to its environment.

Aerobic respiration – respiration using oxygen; releases energy and produces carbon dioxide and water.

Antibody – a protein produced by white blood cells to inactivate disease-causing microorganisms.

Antigen – a marker on the surface of a disease-causing microorganism.

Artery – a blood vessel that carries blood away from the heart.

Artificial insemination – a method of controlling breeding by deliberately selecting suitable parents.

Autotroph – an organism that makes its own food.

Biodiversity – the variety of living organisms in an ecosystem.

Biomass – the mass of living matter in a living organism.

Biosphere – contains all living organisms on Earth.

Biotechnology – the use of organisms, parts of organisms, or the process the organisms carry out, to produce useful (chemical) substances.

Bone – rigid connective tissue that makes up the human skeleton.

Capillary – a blood vessel that connects arteries to veins; where the exchange of materials takes place.

Cartilage – smooth, connecting tissue that covers the ends of bones in a joint.

Cell – the fundamental unit of a living organism.

Central nervous system – the brain and spinal cord; allows an organism to react to its surrounding and coordinates its responses.

Chromosome – a coil of DNA made up of genes, found in the nucleus of plant / animal cells.

Clone – a genetically identical offspring of an organism.

Co-dominant – alleles that are equally dominant; the traits caused by each allele will both appear when both alleles are present.

Commensalism – a symbiotic relationship from which one organism benefits and the other organism is neither harmed nor benefited.

Compensation point – the point at which the rate of photosynthesis exactly matches the rate of respiration.

Decompose – to rot or break down.

Denatured – the state of an enzyme that has been destroyed by heat or pH and can no longer work.

Dislocation – the displacement of a part, especially the displacement of a bone at the joint.

DNA (deoxyribonucleic acid) – the nucleic acid molecules that make up chromosomes and carry genetic information; found in every cell of every organism; control cell chemistry.

Donor – a person who donates blood or an organ.

Effector – the part of the body, e.g. a muscle or a gland, which produces a response to a stimulus.

Embryo – a ball of cells which will develop into a human / animal baby.

Enhanced greenhouse effect – the effect of increasing levels of carbon dioxide in the atmosphere.

Enzyme – a protein molecule and biological catalyst found in living organisms that helps chemical reactions to take place (usually by increasing the rate of reaction).

Evolve – to change naturally over a period of time.

Extinct – a species that has died out.

Fertilisation – the fusion of a male gamete with a female gamete.

Fetus – an unborn animal / human baby.

Food chain – a representation of the feeding relationship between organisms; energy is transferred up the chain.

Fossil fuel – fuel formed in the ground, over millions of years, from the remains of dead plants and animals.

Fuel – a substance that releases energy when burned in the presence of oxygen.

Gamete – a specialised sex cell.

Gene – a small section of DNA, in a chromosome, that determines a particular characteristic; controls cellular activity by providing instructions (coding) for the production of a specific protein.

Glossary

Genetic test – a test to determine if an individual has a genetic disorder.

Genetic modification – the change in the genetic make-up of an organism.

Global warming – the increase in the average temperature on Earth due to a rise in the level of greenhouse gases in the atmosphere.

Greenhouse gas – gases in the Earth's atmosphere that absorb radiation and stop it from leaving the Earth's atmosphere.

Heart – a muscular organ which pumps blood around the body.

Heat stroke – an uncontrolled increase in body temperature.

Heterotroph – an organism that is unable to make its own food; consumes other organisms.

Homeostasis – the maintenance of constant internal conditions in the body.

Hormone – a chemical messenger, made in ductless glands, that travels around the body in the blood to affect target organs elsewhere in the body.

Hypothermia – an uncontrolled decrease in body temperature.

Intensive farming – a method of farming that uses artificial pesticides and fertilizers and controlled environments to maximize food production.

IVF – a technique in which egg cells are fertilised outside the woman's body.

Ligament – the tissue that connects a bone to a joint.

Meiosis – the type of cell division that forms daughter cells with half the number of chromosomes as the parent cell; produces gametes.

Meristem – an area where unspecialised cells divide, producing plant growth, e.g. roots and shoots.

Mitosis – the type of cell division that forms two daughter cells, each with the same number of chromosomes as the parent cell.

Muscle – tissue that can contract and relax to produce movement.

Mutation – a spontaneous change in the genetic material of a cell.

Mutualism – a symbiotic relationship from which both organisms benefit.

Natural selection – the process by which organisms are better adapted to their environment are able to survive and reproduce.

Neuron – a specialised cell that transmits electrical messages (nerve impulses) when stimulated.

Non-biodegradable – a substance that does not decompose naturally by the action of microorganisms.

Non-renewable resources – resources (especially energy sources) that cannot be replaced in a lifetime.

Organic farming – a method of farming that uses natural fertilizers and natural methods of controlling pests with an emphasis on producing quality products.

Osmosis – the net movement of water from a dilute solution (lots of water) to a more concentrated solution (little water) across a partially permeable membrane.

Parasitism – a symbiotic relationship from which one organism benefits and the other organism is harmed.

Pesticide – a chemical used to destroy insects or other pests.

pH – a measure of acidity or alkalinity.

Photosynthesis – the chemical process that takes place in green plants where water combines with carbon dioxide to produce glucose using light energy.

Phototropism – a plant's response to light.

Physiotherapist – a specialist in the treatment of skeletal-muscular injuries.

Pituitary gland – the small gland at the base of the brain that produces hormones.

Plasma – the clear fluid part of blood that contains proteins and minerals.

Platelet – a tiny particle found in blood plasma.

Receptor – the part of the nervous system that detects a stimulus; a sense organ, e.g. eyes, ears, nose, etc.

Recipient – the person receiving a donated organ or blood.

Recycling – to re-use materials that would otherwise be considered waste.

Reflex action – an involuntary action, e.g. automatically jerking your hand away from something hot; a fast, involuntary response to a stimulus.

Renewable – resources (e.g. energy sources) that will not run out or that can be replaced.

Ribosome – a small structure found in the cytoplasm of living cells, where protein synthesis takes place.

Selective breeding – the process by which animals are selected and mated to produce offspring with desirable characteristics (artificial selection).

Specialised – developed or adapted for a specific function.

Species – a group of organisms capable of breeding to produce fertile offspring.

Sprain – a stretch or tear in a ligament.

Symbiosis – a relationship in which members of different species live in close association with one another.

Symptom – a visible or noticeable effect of a disease, illness or injury.

Synapse – the small gap between adjacent neurons.

Tendons – tissue that connects a muscle to a bone.

Ultrasound – sound waves with a very high frequency (above 20 000 Hz).

Vaccine – a liquid preparation used to make the body produce antibodies to provide protection against disease.

Variation – the differences between individuals of the same species.

Vector – an organism (often a microorganism) used to transfer a gene, or genes, from one organism to another.

Veins – a type of blood vessel that transports blood towards the heart.

Wet mass – the mass of a whole, fresh product.

X-ray – an imaging technique that produces shadow pictures of bone and metal.

(HT) Active transport – the movement of substances against a concentration gradient; requires energy.

Auxin – a plant hormone that affects the growth and development of the plant.

Conditioned reflex – a specific reflex response produced when a certain stimulus is detected.

Dry mass – the mass of a dry crop.

Negative feedback – a process when a signal from a receptor instructs an effector to reverse an action.

Osmotic balance – the balance of water entering and leaving a cell.

Pathogen – disease-causing microorganism.

Sickle-cell anaemia – a hereditary blood disorder that affects haemoglobin.

Notes

Acknowledgements

Every effort has been made to contact the holders of copyright material, but if any have been inadvertently overlooked, the publisher will be pleased to make the necessary arrangements at the first opportunity.

The author and publisher would like to thank everyone who has contributed to this book:

p.6   ©iStockphoto.com / Linda Bucklin
p.13   ©iStockphoto.com
          ©iStockphoto.com / Konstantinos Kokkinis
          ©iStockphoto.com / Linda Bucklin
p.15   ©iStockphoto.com
p.18   ©iStockphoto.com / Peter Galbraith
p.24   ©iStockphoto.com / Linda Bucklin
p.43   ©iStockphoto.com
p.45   ©iStockphoto.com / Linda Bucklin
p.55   ©iStockphoto.com / Dawn Hudson
          ©iStockphoto.com / D. Bird, Penfold
p.69   ©iStockphoto.com / Matthew Cole
p.72   ©iStockphoto.com
p.80   ©iStockphoto.com / Patrick Hermans
p.85   ©iStockphoto.com / Stefan Klein
p.87   ©iStockphoto.com

ISBN: 1-978-1-905896-86-8

Published by Lonsdale, a division of Huveaux Plc.

Author: Eliot Attridge

Project Editor: Charlotte Christensen

Cover and concept design: Sarah Duxbury

Designer: Ian Wrigley

Artwork: HL Studios

Author Information

Dr Eliot Attridge is a full member of the Institute of Biology, a chartered biologist CBiol, and an experienced Head of Science. He works closely with the exam board as an Assistant Examiner for Twenty First Century Science and was involved in writing the scheme of work for the new GCSE. His school, having been involved in the pilot, is now implementing the new GCSE.

Index